best | designed

Martin Nicholas Kunz

wellness hotels

NORTH AND SOUTH AMERICA . CARIBBEAN . MEXICO
NORD- UND SÜDAMERIKA . KARIBIK . MEXIKO

Second updated edition
2. aktualisierte Auflage

avedition

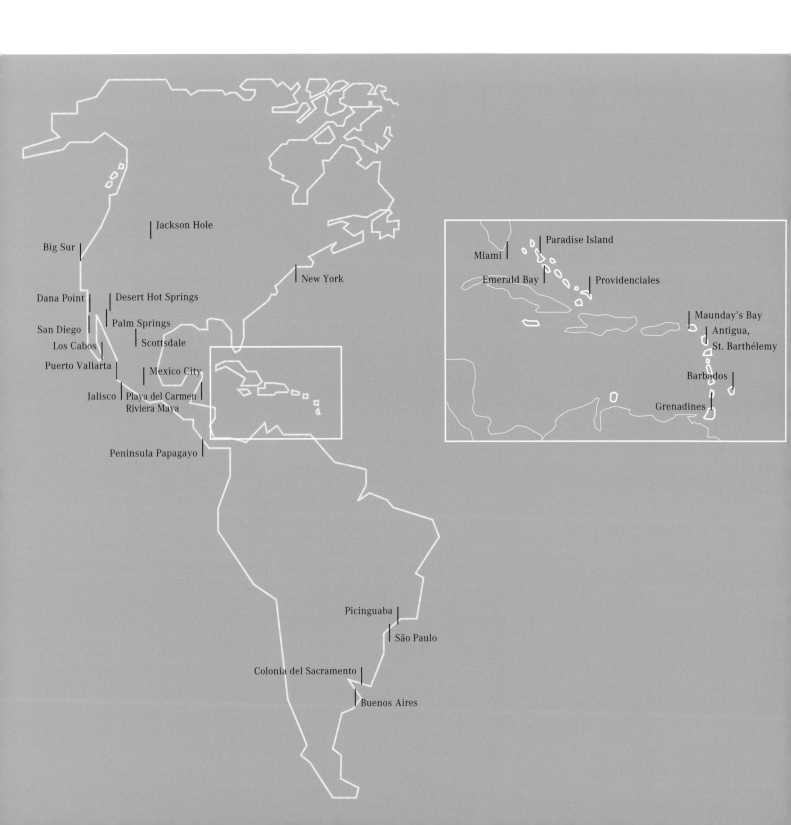

Jackson Hole

Big Sur

New York

Dana Point | Desert Hot Springs

San Diego | Palm Springs

Los Cabos | Scottsdale

Puerto Vallarta

Jalisco | Mexico City

Playa del Carmen
Riviera Maya

Peninsula Papagayo

Picinguaba

São Paulo

Colonia del Sacramento

Buenos Aires

Miami | Paradise Island

Emerald Bay | Providenciales

Maunday's Bay

Antigua,
St. Barthélemy

Barbados

Grenadines

01 02

"Simply beautiful." That is the way you could summarize the hotels illustrated on the following 168 pages. Take a moment to let the photos sink in. Begin to dream what it would be like to lie on a teak lounge chair on the white sand and look out over the ocean to the horizon. Or imagine breathing in the scent of the ocean waters at dawn, waking up in the contrast baths between the salty spray and the fresh water infinity pool. Or meditating in the shade of a palm tree, having your tired neck muscles gently massaged by experienced hands. Perhaps going to the travel agency or surfing the next website, looking for flights. The hotels awaken desires, but also expectations. Naturally, they are always part of an inspiration: the photographer's subjective view and the graphic designer's click on the computer to compose the images. Should they emphasize something other than the crème de la crème? Should they put something else together on these pages, besides captivating perspectives and outstanding architectural details? Of course, the pictures intentionally appeal to our feelings and desires. Each of these hotels tells another story, has its own individual soul. We can't begin to tell about the cuisine you cannot taste, about the scented flowers you cannot smell. The sounds you cannot hear, the surroundings and the adventurous trips to the hotel you cannot see, or the wellness experiences you can get an impression of when turning the pages of a book, but cannot feel for yourself. You could go on and on about all the

03 04

positive surprises you experience on the trip to all these locations—yet at the same time, you should not try to cover up any faults. First of all, let us name a few of the wonderful details: for example, the extremely informal atmosphere at Rhoni and Cristina's Sagewater Spa is highly recommended. You could also talk about the retro furnishings of Hope Springs. About the swimming pool's smooth-as-glass surface at the Amangani; the rooftop bar on the Habita; the spa-whirlpool surrounded by candles at the Ikal

del Mar; or the no-electricity philosophy of the Hotelito Desconocido. However, we do not want to give away all of the details right from the start. There are still a few more pages to look at. And in the end? Despite the faults and flaws—the pictures prevail, on paper and in reality. Harmony of the senses: Simply beautiful, you will see.

01 | Mandarin Oriental, New York

02 | Le Sereno

03 | St. Regis Resort, Monarch Beach

04 | Kempinski Hotel Colony Park Plaza

05   06

Sie sind einfach schön! So könnte man die auf den folgenden 168 Seiten dargestellten Hotels in einem Satz zusammenfassen. Die Fotos auf sich wirken lassen. Zu Träumen beginnen, ausmalen wie es wäre, läge man auf einem der Teakholz-liegestühl im weißen Sand und schaute über den Ozean in den Horizont. Oder man stelle sich vor, den Duft des Meerwassers in der Morgen-dämmerung einzuatmen, in Wechselbädern zwischen salziger Gischt und kantenlosen Süß-wasserbecken aufzuwachen. Im Schatten einer Palme zu meditieren, sich von geübten Händen den steifen Nacken kneten zu lassen. Ins Reise-büro gehen oder auf die nächste Website surfen, nach Flügen schauen... Sie wecken Sehnsüchte, aber auch Erwartungen. Natürlich sind sie immer auch Teil einer Inszenierung. Ein subjektiver Blick der Fotografen und komponierender Klick der Grafikdesigner. Was sonst sollten sie auch hervorkehren als die „Schokoladenseiten". Was sonst sollten sie auf den Seiten zusammenfü-gen, als in den Bann ziehende Perspektiven und architektonisch herausragende Details? Natürlich sprechen die Bilder mit voller Absicht unsere Gefühle und Wünsche an. Jedes dieser Häuser erzählt aber auch eine Geschichte, hat seinen individuellen Geist. Wir wollen über das Essen, das man nicht schmecken kann, berichten, über die Düfte der Pflanzen, die man nicht riechen kann. Die Geräusche, die man nicht hören kann, die Umgebung und teilweise abenteuerlichen Anfahrten, die man nicht sehen kann oder die Wellness-Erlebnisse, die man

07 08

beim Blättern durch das Buch ahnt, aber nicht selbst fühlen kann. Es ließe sich endlos von all den positiven Überraschungen erzählen, die man auf der Reise an all diese Orte entdeckt. Zuerst seien aber ein paar der wunderbaren Details genannt: Erwähnenswert ist zum Beispiel die überaus familiäre Atmosphäre bei Rhoni und Cristina im Sagewater Spa. Zu plaudern wäre über die Retro-Ausstattung des Hope Springs, über das einer spiegelglatten Eisbahn ähnliche Schwimmbecken im Amangani oder die Bar

auf dem Dach des Habita, der kerzenumstellte Spa-Whirlpool im Ikal del Mar und die ohne-Strom-Philosophie des Hotelito Desconocido. Doch wir wollen ja nicht alle Details gleich zu Anfang verraten. Es gibt ja noch ein paar Seiten mehr. Und am Ende? Trotz Brüchen und Macken – am Ende siegen die Bilder, auf dem Papier und in Wirklichkeit. Harmonie der Sinne: Einfach schön! Sie werden sehen.

amangani | jackson hole . wyoming

DESIGN: Edward Tuttle

The peaks of the Rocky Mountains stretch upward toward the sky to the left and the right of the plateau on which the Amangani was built. The hotel that is located beside the plains and forest that are a haven for animals threatened by extinction. However, this is not only an escape for the animals: In the language of the Native American Shoshone tribe, Amangani means "peaceful home". This hotel in Northwestern Wyoming is an honor to its name. The structure fits into the mountainous environment, forests and grasslands by using natural materials. The warm tones of stone from Oklahoma, Douglas Fir, cedar and Pacific Redwood dominate the appearance both on the interior as well as the exterior. A heated swimming pool with whirlpool and a view of the Teton Range mountain chain make it possible to swim outdoors even in the winter. The hotel has 40 suites available for its guests. All of these rooms are furnished with a comfortable bathroom and a spacious living room. There you may enjoy the fire in the fireplace framed in dark iron and lounge in the chairs covered in cowhide. The dark cedar beams on the ceiling and walls, as well as art collections made of stretched hides or untreated woods, give the impression of a comfortable yet exclusively-furnished wigwam.

Links und rechts der Hochebene, auf der das Amangani gebaut wurde, recken sich die Gipfel der Rocky Mountains auf. Das Hotel mitten in den bekanntesten Bergen Nordamerikas befindet sich in unmittelbarer Nähe zu Weideflächen und Waldgebieten, die ein Refugium für selten gewordene Tiere sind. Doch nicht nur die Tiere können sich in dieser Gegend zurückziehen: Amangani bedeutet in der Sprache der Schoschonen-Indianer „friedvolles Heim". Diesem Namen macht das Hotel im Nordwesten von Wyoming alle Ehre. Der Bau fügt sich durch die Verwendung natürlicher Materialien bruchlos in die Umgebung von Gebirge, Wäldern und Grasland ein. Die warmen Töne von Sandstein aus Oklahoma, Douglas-Tanne, Zedernholz und pazifischem Redwood bestimmen das Erscheinungsbild von außen wie innen. Ein wohltemperiertes Schwimmbecken mit Whirlpool und Blick auf die Gebirgskette von Teton Range erlaubt es selbst im Winter, sich draußen im Wasser aufzuhalten. 40 Suiten hält das Haus für seine Gäste bereit. Alle diese Zimmer sind mit einem komfortablen Bad und einem großzügigen Wohnzimmer ausgestattet. Dort bietet sich auch die Möglichkeit, den mit patiniertem dunklem Eisen gerahmten Kamin anzufeuern und sich auf den mit Kuhhaut bezogenen Sesseln zu lümmeln. Dunkle Zedernholzplanken an der Decke und den Wänden sowie Kunstensembles aus gespannten Fellen oder rohen Hölzern lassen den Eindruck eines ebenso wohligen wie exklusiven Wigwams entstehen.

01 | Even worth the trip in the winter: the Amangani near the Rocky Mountains.

Auch im Winter eine Reise wert: das Amangani nahe der Rocky Mountains.

03 04

02 | Guests of the Amangani can enjoy the view while swimming in
the warm waters of the pool.

Im wohlig warmen Wasser des Pools schwimmend können die
Gäste des Amangani den Blick auf die Rocky Mountains genießen.

03 | The „peaceful home" not only warms the body with its fireplace
but also the heart.

Das „friedvolle Heim" wärmt mit seinen Kaminfeuern nicht nur
den Körper, sondern auch die Herzen der Gäste.

04 | No one has to remain alone for long in the Amangani: Guests may
gather, if they like, in the large lounge with a fireplace.

Im Amangani muss niemand lang allein bleiben: Im
Kaminzimmer kommt man ungezwungen zusammen.

st. regis resort, monarch beach | dana point . california
DESIGN: Hirsch Bedner Associates of Santa Monica, California; Holmes & Narver of Orange, California

This hotel relocates Italy from the Mediterranean Sea to the Pacific Ocean. The various buildings of the complex are built in the Tuscany style so that from one building to the next the guest feels as if he/she is on an Italian piazza. But in order to keep guests from getting lazy from all the relaxation, St. Regis Resort, Monarch Beach offers a golf course with a view of the open ocean. The Pacific waves hit the shore and the golfers can hit their balls to the best of their ability to come as close as possible to the next hole. For those who forget their clubs at home or decide to start their golf career at the spur of the moment, guests can acquire all the necessary utensils at the hotel pro shop. A fitness center, tennis courts, and the hotel pool, in addition to the golf course, will keep guests moving. Guests can relax in the St. Regis Spa, in which waterfalls and fountains lull visitors into a little beauty sleep. One might think that this is not quite the place for a vacation with the kids. Think again! In the "Sandcastle Club", children are supervised by qualified caregivers and can learn the art of sandcastle building and searching of shells, wave riding, or take their first steps on the tennis court. If you have a bundle of energy on your hands, let him/her try a few salutes to the sun in the children's yoga class and thus make the relaxation a long-lasting effect.

Dieses Hotel verlegt Italien vom Mittelmeer an den Pazifischen Ozean. Die verschiedenen Gebäude der Anlage sind im Toskana-Stil errichtet, so dass der Gast unterwegs vom einen zum anderen Haus des Hotels sich wie auf einer italienischen Piazza fühlt. Damit die Besucher vor lauter Erholung nicht träge werden, bietet das St. Regis Resort, Monarch Beach einen Golfplatz mit Blick auf das offene Meer. Die Pazifikwellen schlagen an den Strand und die Golfer ihre Bälle je nach Können so nah wie möglich zum nächsten Loch. Wer seinen Schläger zu Hause vergessen hat oder sich spontan entschlossen hat, eine Golfkarriere zu starten, kann sich im hauseigenen Golfshop mit allen nötigen Utensilien eindecken. Neben dem Golfplatz laden aber auch ein Fitness-Studio, Tennisplätze und der Hotelpool dazu ein, in Bewegung zu bleiben. Vollends abschalten können die Gäste im St. Regis Spa, in dem Wasserfälle und Brunnen die Besucher in einen kleinen Schönheitsschlaf wispern. Nicht der beste Ort für einen Urlaub mit Kind, könnte man nun denken. Aber weit gefehlt: Im Sandcastle Club können Kinder unter Aufsicht von Betreuern die Kunst des Sandburgenbauens und Muschelsuchens erlernen, Wellenreiten oder ihre ersten Versuche auf dem Tennisplatz wagen. Und wer zu Hause einen Zappelphillip sitzen hat, kann diesen beim Kinderyoga ein paar Sonnengrüße ausprobieren lassen, und so die Entspannung zu einem bleibenden Zustand machen.

01 | You would almost expect to hear "Azzuro" coming from the sound system: the hotel pool.

Fast würde man erwarten, aus jedem Lautsprecher „Azzuro" zu hören: der Hotelpool.

02 | The inner courtyard equals any real Mediterranean passage—the only things missing are the stray dogs.

Der Innenhof steht einer echten mediterranen Passage kaum nach – allein die streunenden Hunde fehlen.

03 | The rooms offer enough space for two—or three: At the St. Regis Resort, Monarch Beach there is a great emphasis on making a comfortable stay for families.

Die Zimmer bieten genug Platz für zwei – oder drei: Im St. Regis Resort, Monarch Beach legt man großen Wert darauf, Familien einen angenehmen Aufenthalt zu bereiten.

04 | The entire hotel combines a confident European style with American comfort.

Das gesamte Hotel verbindet europäisches Stilbewusstsein mit amerikanischem Komfort.

05 | In addition to precious marble, you will also find bath accessories by Remède in the bathrooms. All of the furniture is specially made for the hotel.

Edler Marmor findet sich auch in den mit Remède-Kosmetika ausgestatteten Badezimmern. Alle Möbel sind Spezialanfertigungen für das Hotel.

04

03 05

01 | See and—not be seen: absolute tranquility at the Post Ranch.

Sehen und - nicht gesehen werden: absolute Ruhe in der Post Ranch.

post ranch inn | big sur . california

DESIGN: Mickey Muennig, Janet Gay Freed

Long ago before the first settlers at the Big Sur discovered "their new paradise", the Esalen and Salinas Indians were already bathing in the natural pools served by the hot springs between the cliffs and the Pacific Ocean. Furthermore, the area became a kind of "birthplace" for the New Age movement and even today, with the Esalen Institute, is a center for holistic medicine. The great-grandson of the founder, William Brainward Post, still leads many of the guided nature hikes for the hotel. At the end of the 80's, Mike Freed and Mickey Muennig, developed the idea to build a hotel directly above the Pacific surge. Of course, this was not to be just any hotel, but the realization of a dream and the combination of sophisticated architecture and the natural experience. The architect, Mickey Muennig, is a follower of the ecological architectural movement. He divided up the 30 guestrooms, restaurant, spa, fitness rooms, library, boutique and reception on the compound in various building concepts with a maximum of three living units. Upon arrival, one hardly sees the entire complex spreading over the 98 acres of the hotel area. The Post Ranch Inn offers five different types of room designs: ocean, coast, tree, butterfly and mountain houses. The interior of all the buildings on the Post Ranch are extremely spacious and they have a calming geometric effect using their combinations of materials: wood, glass, stone and concrete.

Schon einige Zeit bevor die ersten Siedler am Big Sur „ihr neues Paradies" entdeckten, badeten die Esalen- und Salinas- Indianer in den durch heiße Quellen gespeisten Naturpools zwischen Klippen und Pazifischem Ozean. Zudem war die Gegend eine Art Keimzelle für die New Age-Bewegung und bildet noch heute mit dem Esalen Institute ein Zentrum für ganzheitliche Medizin. Der Urenkel des Gründers William Brainward Post führt heute noch Naturwandertouren durch. Mike Freed und Mickey Muennig entwickelten Ende der 80er Jahre die Idee, direkt oberhalb der pazifischen Brandung ein Hotel zu errichten. Freilich sollte es nicht irgendeine Herberge sein, sondern die Verwirklichung eines Traums und die Kombination aus anspruchsvoller Architektur und Naturerlebnis. Der Architekt Mickey Muennig ist ein Anhänger ökologischer Bauweise. Dieser verteilte die 30 Gästezimmer, Restaurant, Spa, Fitnessräume, Bibliothek, Boutique und Rezeption verstreut auf dem Gelände in ganz unterschiedliche Gebäudekonzepte mit maximal drei Wohneinheiten. Die gesamte Anlage ist bei der Anfahrt auf das rund 36 Hektar große Hotelareal so gut wie unsichtbar. Fünf verschiedene Zimmertypen bietet das Post Ranch Inn: Ocean, Coast, Tree, Butterfly und Mountain Houses. Im Innern sind alle Gebäude der Post Ranch extrem geräumig und mit ihrer Materialkombination aus Holz, Glas, Stein und Beton von beruhigender Geometrie.

02 | Special attention was always paid when planning the hotel that it was built ecologically-friendly and using natural materials.

Bei der Planung der Hotelzimmer wurde stets darauf geachtet, umweltfreundlich zu bauen und natürliche Materialien zu verwenden.

03 | Stone, water, sea, sky—the environment of the Post Ranch Spa changes in the colors. Here you can again become one with yourself and with nature.

Stein, Wasser, Meer, Himmel - in den Farben Grau und Blau changiert die Umgebung des Post Ranch Spa. Hier wird man wieder eins mit sich selbst und der Natur.

04 | After taking the first step out of bed in the morning, your mind will be clear observing the panoramic view of the sea.

Schon nach dem ersten Schritt aus dem Bett am frühen Morgen wird der Kopf frei bei dem weiten Blick auf das Meer.

05 | Thanks to the open structure of the building, even when in the spa, you have the feeling of being in the luxurious accommodations of a nature park ranger.

Die offene Struktur des Gebäudes lässt sogar im Spa das Gefühl entstehen, man befinde sich in einer luxuriösen Unterkunft eines Naturpark-Rangers.

01 | Retro charm: The furniture comes from antique stores and from ebay.

Retro-Charme: Die Möbel stammen aus Antiquitätenläden und von E-Bay.

hope springs | desert hot springs . california

DESIGN: Steve & Misako Samiof, Mike Haggerty

Near White Water where Freeway 10 leads off into the desert, you turn right to go on Highway 111 to one of America's largest golf and senior citizen paradises. Mick Haggerty, a desert lover and graphic designer, as well as Steve and Misako Samiof, are among the pioneers who opened up this area for the younger generation. In 1999 the opportunity presented itself to acquire the fairly worn-out Cactus Spring Motel and they completely renovated the 10 room property dating from the year 1958. Now the walls and ceilings are mostly in light green and yellow tones, the floors are all made of beveled and polished cement. They found the furniture in antique stores or in ebay auctions. The water for the three hotel pools comes completely from the hot springs, and while the larger pool with 95 degrees Fahrenheit is also suitable for swimming, the temperature in the covered third pool rises to 105 degrees Fahrenheit. In contrast to the mostly opulent gardens with colorful shrubs, cacti and stones, the spacious rooms are furnished in an extremely purist fashion with futon-like beds, well-lit bathrooms, a few lights and also some shelves and clothing hooks. Hope Springs offers complete isolation and thus there are no telephones or television in the rooms, but they do have a CD player and a small library with an exquisite jazz selection.

In der Nähe von White Water, wo der Freeway 10 in die Wüste hinab führt, geht es rechts auf der Bundesstraße 111 in eines der größten amerikanischen Golf- und Rentnerparadiese. Zu den Pionieren, die diese Gegend wieder einem jüngeren Publikum erschlossen haben, zählen die Graphikdesigner und Wüsten-Liebhaber Mick Haggerty sowie Steve und Misako Samiof. 1999 bot sich ihnen die Möglichkeit, das bereits reichlich abgewohnte Cactus Spring Motel zu ergattern, und so entrümpelten sie das 10-Zimmer-Anwesen aus dem Jahre 1958 komplett. Die Wand- und Deckenflächen sind nun größtenteils in zarten Gelb- und Grüntönen, die Fußböden durchgehend aus geschliffenem und poliertem Zement. Das Mobiliar suchten sie sich in Antiquitätenläden oder ersteigerten es auf Ebay. Das Wasser der drei Hotelpools stammt komplett aus den heißen Quellen und während der größere Pool mit rund 35 °C auch zum Schwimmen geeignet ist, steigert sich die Temperatur in dem überdachten, dritten Pool bis zu 40,5 °C. Im Gegensatz zum eher üppigen Garten mit farbigen Büschen, Kakteen und Steinen sind die geräumigen Zimmer äußerst puristisch mit futonähnlichen Betten, hellen Bädern, einigen wenigen Leuchten und ein paar Fachböden und Kleiderhaken ausgestattet. Hope Springs bietet völlige Abgeschiedenheit und so gibt es in den Zimmern weder Telefon noch TV, dafür aber einen CD-Player und eine kleine Bibliothek mit erlesener Jazzmusik.

02   03

02 | Nothing harsh about the desert here; when your goal is Hope Springs, that is. The hotel pool does not offer much cooling off, but it is perfect for relaxing in the desert waters.

Jeder wird gern in die Wüste geschickt, wenn das Ziel Hope Springs ist. Der Hotelpool bietet zwar keine Abkühlung, aber Entspannung im Wüstenwasser.

03 | The furnishings are reduced to a minimum—that may appear Spartanic to some; for others it is pleasantly uncluttered.

Die Einrichtung ist auf ein Minimum reduziert - dem einen mag das spartanisch erscheinen, für die anderen ist es wohltuend entrümpelt.

04 | The hearth is an ideal place to chat with the other guests. Someone is sure to remember a campfire song or two.

Die Feuerstelle ist ein idealer Ort, um mit den anderen Gästen ins Gespräch zu kommen. Manch einer hat auch sicher noch ein Lagerfeuerlied im Kopf.

05 | In the past, Hope Springs was a motel—today everyone would like to stay for more than just one night.

Früher war das Hope Springs ein Motel - heute wünscht sich jeder, länger als nur eine Nacht zu bleiben.

sagewater spa | desert hot springs . california

DESIGN: Rhoni Epstein, Cristina Pestana

From the outside, the Sagewater with its seven rooms, is so small that you could almost overlook it. It lies well secluded in the small Eliseo Road. The seven rooms of the former motel, managed today by Rhoni Epstein and Cristina Pestana, almost give you the feeling that you are visiting two of your aunts. At the latest when you are relaxing in the warm waters of the pool, you begin a new calculation of time. The reason for that is presumably the healing effect of the desert water. After a long trip through the San Andreas Valley, it springs forth in the middle of the desert at an almost boiling 165 degrees Fahrenheit, completely pure and enriched with valuable minerals from the depths of the earth. In the Sagewater, the water is allowed to cool off to 105 degrees Fahrenheit and is constantly pumped into the smaller, warm water pool and at 90 degrees Fahrenheit into the actual swimming pool. The rooms feel very well ventilated thanks to the typical California "Mid-Century" architecture and its seamless transitions between indoors and outdoors. From the inner courtyard and its surrounding desert landscape, they are only separated by glass, screens or wide, white blinds. It is not unusual for the temperatures to reach around 104 degrees Fahrenheit in July and August. If your are expecting scorching hot heat in Desert Hot Springs, you might be disappointed, because in addition to a subtle air conditioning system, a light breeze blows across the estate all year long. Especially on the weekends, a growing number of guests from as far as Los Angeles visit the Sagewater.

Das Sagewater mit seinen sieben Zimmern ist von außen so klein, dass man es glatt übersieht. Gut versteckt liegt es in der kleinen Eliseo Road. Die sieben Zimmer des ehemaligen Motels, das heute von Rhoni Epstein und Cristina Pestana geführt wird, lassen beinahe das Gefühl aufkommen, man sei bei zwei guten Tanten zu Besuch. Spätestens im wohlig warmen Wasser des Pools beginnt eine Art neuer Zeitrechnung. Grund dafür ist vermutlich die heilende Wirkung des Wüstenwassers. Nach einer langen Reise durch den Sankt-Andreas-Graben sprudelt es hier inmitten der Wüste fast kochend heiß mit 70 °C, vollkommen rein und mit wertvollen Mineralien angereichert, aus der Tiefe. Im Sagewater wird es auf 46 °C heruntergekühlt und ins kleinere Warmbecken ständig frisch eingepumpt und mit 35 °C ins eigentliche Schwimmbad. Die Räume wirken dank der typisch kalifornischen Mid-Century-Architektur und deren nahtlosen Übergängen zwischen außen und innen sehr luftig. Vom Innenhof und der umliegenden Wüstenlandschaft sind sie nur durch Glas, Fliegengitter oder breite, weiße Rollos getrennt. Im Juli oder August sind Temperaturen um die 45 °C keine Seltenheit. Wer allerdings in Desert Hot Springs besonders glühende Hitze erwartet, wird enttäuscht, denn neben einer unaufdringlichen Klimatisierung kühlt auch ein Lüftchen ganzjährig das Anwesen. Vor allem an den Wochenenden besucht der inzwischen weit über Los Angeles hinaus angewachsene Gästekreis das Sagewater.

01 | Classical mid-century architecture defines the entire hotel complex.

Klassische Mid-Century-Architektur bestimmt die gesamte Hotelanlage.

02 | In the Sagewater, the guests can dream the dream along with the owners
Cristina Pestana and Rhoni Epstein: A spa in the middle of the desert.

Im Sagewater können die Gäste den Traum der Besitzerinnen Cristina Pestana
und Rhoni Epstein mitträumen: ein Spa mitten in der Wüste.

03 | The rooms are enclosed in glass on only one side so that the cool breeze that blows all year round can give the rooms a breath of fresh air.

Die Zimmer sind jeweils zu einer Seite weitgehend verglast, so dass der kühlende Wind, der ganzjährig weht, die Räume stets mit frischer Luft versorgt.

04 | The pool that lies beneath the ever-brilliant blue sky is filled with cooled-off desert water that has healing properties thanks to its minerals.

Der Pool unter stets strahlend blauem Himmel wird mit heruntergekühltem Wüstenwasser befüllt, das dank seiner Mineralien Heilkräfte besitzt.

01 | A campfire for distinguished cowboys: The garden of Parker's Palm Springs.

Lagerfeuer für distinguierte Cowboys: der Garten des Parker's Palm Springs.

the parker palm springs | palm springs . california
DESIGN: David Mann, Jonathan Adler

A hotel that has its own "Gene Autry" suite and whose spa has been declared as adult entertainment for adults cannot be a bad place. Fans of the singing cowboy can either check into the suite named in his honor or book another of the other so-called "villas" in the complex of The Parker Palm Springs. Those who prefer the shortest way to the bar and restaurant will enjoy one of the junior suites. All of the rooms in the hotel have a number of styles and epochs—the hotel that is rich in tradition has constantly been adapted to meet the guests needs. In the Parker Palm Springs, there is never a problem with a little extravaganza here and there, after all, the spa called PSYC has a solid single malt whiskey in its manifest under the category of Sports and Fitness. Those who have partaken of this will enjoy a nice, old-fashioned type of sports such as croquet and petanque that are almost more fun under the palms of Palm Springs than on the sacred English lawns or the dusty French village squares. Languishing from all the retro-activities? Guests may select between Norma's and Mister Parker's: Without even batting an eye, Norma's offers an outstanding breakfast or lunch until 3 pm; whereas Mister Parker's has specialized itself in the evening culinary explosions.

Ein Hotel, das über eine Gene Autry-Suite verfügt und seinen Spabereich als Adult Entertainment deklariert, kann kein schlechter Ort sein. Verehrer des singenden Cowboys können entweder in die nach ihm benannten Zwei-Zimmer-Apartments einchecken oder aber eines der anderen „Villa" genannten Behausung auf dem Anwesen des The Parker Palm Springs mieten. Wer einen kürzeren Weg zur Bar und zum Restaurant bevorzugt, ist mit einer der Junior-Suiten bestens bedient. Alle Räume des Hotels zitieren eine Vielzahl von Stilen und Zeiten – das traditionsreiche Haus wurde mit der Zeit stets behutsam den Ansprüchen seiner Gäste angeglichen. Im Parker's hat man keine Probleme mit einer kleinen Extravaganz hier und da, schließlich führt das PSYC genannte Spa in seinem Manifest in der Rubrik Sport und Fitness auch einen soliden Single Malt Whiskey auf. Wer diesen eingenommen hat, wird auch an den sympathisch altmodischen Sportarten Croquet und Petanque Gefallen finden, die unter den Palmen von Palm Springs beinahe noch mehr Spaß machen als auf heiligem englischen Rasen und staubigen französischen Dorfplätzen. Ermattet von so viel Retro-Aktivität darf der Gast zwischen dem Norma's und dem Mister Parker's wählen: Im Norma's bietet man ohne mit der Wimper zu zucken bis 15 Uhr ein hervorragendes Frühstück und auch Lunch an, während man sich im Mister Parker's auf abendliche Geschmacksexplosionen spezialisiert hat.

02 | The door at the Parker Palm Springs is always open, even at night—after all they are specialized in entertainment.

Auch nachts steht die Tür des Parker's Palm Springs immer offen – schließlich ist man hier auf Entertainment spezialisiert.

03 | The exterior of the bungalows at the Parker are subtle. A tactic by the designer: the interior design is always a pleasant surprise.

Von außen sind die Bungalows des Parker's nicht besonders auffallend. Ein kluger Zug der Designer: die Inneneinrichtung wird so immer zu einem Überraschungserfolg.

04 | At the Parker Palm Springs everything reminds you of the wild 60's—only better. The interior is constantly cared for and lovingly renovated.

Im Parker's ist noch alles wie in den wilden 60ern – nur besser. Das Interieur wurde kontinuierlich gepflegt und behutsam renoviert.

05 | Instead of cold and unfriendly hyper-design, Parker's offers guests staged eclecticism.

Statt unterkühltem Hyper-Design bietet man den Gästen gekonnt inszenierten Eklektizismus.

03 04

05

06 | While the atmosphere in other hotels is often humorless, in every corner of Parkers there are hip, little details that make you smile.

Während man sich in anderen Hotels in humorfreien Zonen wähnt, findet man im Parker's an jeder Ecke ein kleines Detail, das einen schmunzeln lässt.

07 | In this spa, every woman feels like a beauty queen from the 50's—even Marilyn Monroe loved Parker's.

In diesem Spa darf sich jede Frau wie eine 50er Jahre Schönheitskönigin fühlen – auch Marilyn Monroe hätte das Parker's geliebt.

08 | The staff pays careful attention to the smallest details.

Selbst auf kleinste Details wird hier geachtet.

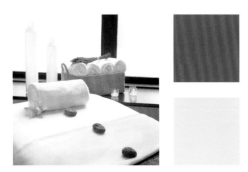

w san diego | san diego . california

DESIGN: Jensen-Fey Architecture & Planning, Shopworks in collaboration with W Design Group

First class service, central location and an attractive interior is simply expected from better business hotels today. The W Hotels are nevertheless unusual for a business hotel chain. Guests will notice immediately that the W San Diego is not just any run of the mill hotel. Individual design, comfortable lounges and modern office technology offer space to concentrate on working as well as an opportunity to unwind at the end of a long day. The suites have their own living room to relax in after a hard day's work. According to the management, the W stands for warm, witty and wonderful. W could just as well stand for "woof". Because in the W San Diego, as well as in all the other hotels in the chain, our four-legged friends are also welcome guests. They have even designed their own lounge and entertainment program for dogs and cats. At the check in, there is a "welcome package" including toys and a tag for the collar. There are pet beds and feeding dishes in the rooms. Of course, there is also a dog-walking service. The extra services cost Fido's master a small fee plus cleaning costs, but after all, he is man's best friend.

Erstklassiger Service, zentrale Lage und ein ansprechendes Interieur wird heutzutage von jedem besseren Businesshotel erwartet. Trotzdem sind die W Hotels für eine Businesshotelkette doch eher unüblich. Und diese Erkenntnis springt dem Gast auch im W San Diego ins Auge. Individuelles Design, gemütliche Lounges und moderne Bürotechnik bieten Raum für konzentriertes Arbeiten, aber eben auch Gelegenheit für Muße und den wohlverdienten Feierabend. Nach einem arbeitsreichen Tag soll der Gast entspannen, wie im eigenen Wohnzimmer. Dies kann er im privaten Rahmen seiner Suite oder in einem der angesagten Hotelrestaurants tun. Laut Management steht das W für warm, witzig, und wunderbar. W könnte aber genauso gut für „wuff" stehen. Denn im W San Diego, wie übrigens in allen Häusern der Kette, sind auch Vierbeiner willkommene Gäste. Für Hund und Katz wird sogar ein eigenes Aufenthalts- und Unterhaltungsprogramm entworfen. Beim Check-in gibt es ein Willkommenspaket inklusive Spielzeug und Halsbandanhänger. Im Zimmer warten Körbchen und Fressnapf. Und ein Gassi-Geh-Service versteht sich von selbst. Das alles gibt's für den Hund gegen einen kleinen Aufpreis vom Herrchen, zuzüglich Reinigungsgebühr.

01 | The business hotel in Downtown San Diego has 258 rooms and 5 conference rooms.
Das Businesshotel in Downtown San Diego hat 258 Zimmer und 5 Tagungsräume.

02 | The motto is modern but comfortable. Most of the furniture is handcrafted.

Das Motto lautet modern, aber gemütlich. Viele der Möbel sind handgefertigt.

03 | In the Anatomy Spa or the fitness center with a personal trainer, you can forget about the day's stress.

Abschalten vom Business kann man im Anatomy Spa oder im Fitness-Center mit einem Personal Trainer.

04 | The first W Hotel was opened in 1998 in New York. There are now more than 20 hotels world wide.

1998 wurde in New York das erste W Hotel eröffnet. Inzwischen gibt es mehr als 20 Häuser weltweit.

05 | If you are sleepless in San Diego, then snuggle into the down blankets covered in Egyptian cotton linens.

Wer in San Diego Zeit zum Schlafen findet, der tut das hier, eingehüllt in Gänsedaunen und ägyptisches Leinen.

06 | Every room has its own coffee machine with the special W-coffee blend.

Jedes Zimmer hat eine eigene Kaffeemaschine mit der speziellen W-Kaffeemischung.

04 05

06

sanctuary on camelback mountain | scottsdale . arizona

DESIGN: Hiriam Hudson Benedict, Catherine M. Hayes of Hayes

This boutique retreat offers a dramatic view of the mountain scenery in the Camelback Mountains. The small spa casitas are spread out on over 53 acres in the exotic desert landscape of the northern foothills of the mountains. They were built in the 50's by Hiriam Hudson Benedict, one of Frank Lloyd Wright's students. The complex was used in the late 60's mainly as a tennis club as the hotel's five championship tennis courts remind us. Another center also invites us to fitness training, in which, besides pilates, guests can also participate in yoga and meditation courses. After an extensive session in the spa, guests can stroll through the meditation garden that also serves to guide us to inner contemplation. The Sanctuary on Camelback Mountain is also specialized in weddings and gatherings of any kind. The staff understands that even a business meeting does not necessarily have to be stressful. Although you might ask yourself, given the grandeur of the nearby mountains and the many beguiling diversions, how can any work ever get done? Those are the worries of the privileged who are lucky enough to visit the Sanctuary on Camelback Mountain on such a special occasion.

Dieses Boutique-Refugium bietet eine Aussicht auf die dramatische Bergkulisse der Camelback Mountains. Die kleinen Spa-Häuser liegen auf über 21 Hektar verteilt in exotischer Wüstenlandschaft der nördlichen Ausläufer der Berge. Gebaut wurden sie in den 50er Jahren von Hiriam Hudson Benedict, einem Schüler Frank Lloyd Wrights. Die Anlage wurde in den späten sechziger Jahren vor allem als Tennisclub genutzt, daran erinnern auch noch heute die fünf Tennisplätze des Hotels auf Turnierniveau. Zum Fitnesstraining lädt zusätzlich auch noch ein Studio ein, in dem neben Pilates- auch Yoga- und Meditationskurse belegt werden können. Der inneren Einkehr dient auch der Meditationsgarten, durch den man nach einer ausgedehnten Spasitzung wandeln kann. Sanctuary on Camelback hat sich zusätzlich auch auf Hochzeiten und Zusammenkünfte aller Art spezialisiert. Man hat hier verinnerlicht, dass selbst ein Arbeitsmeeting kein Stress sein muss. Es fragt sich allerdings, wie angesichts der Erhabenheit der nahen Berge und der vielen verführerischen Ablenkungen des Hotels überhaupt ein Arbeitsklima entstehen soll – doch das mag die Sorge der Glücklichen sein, die das Sanctuary on Camelback zu so einem Anlass aufsuchen dürfen.

01 | The rugged beauty of the surroundings is reflected in the material used for the building.

Die raue Schönheit der Umgebung spiegelt sich in den für den Bau verwendeten Materialien wider.

02 03
04

05

02 | Only a shower in the rain could be more natural than the bathrooms in Sanctuary on Camelback Mountain.

Nur eine Dusche im Regen könnte naturverbundener sein als die Badezimmer im Sanctuary on Camelback.

03 | Living area in one of the spa casitas.

Wohnbereich in einem der Spa Häuser.

04 | They intentionally saved when furnishing the complex, all the colorful kitsch was avoided, only simple elegance defines all areas of the hotel.

Bei der Einrichtung der Anlage wurde gespart: Auf alles Billig-Bunte wurde verzichtet, nur Schlicht-Schönes findet sich in allen Bereichen des Hotels.

05 | The spa invites guests to relax after a workout on the tennis courts or the fitness center.

Nach einer Trainingseinheit auf dem Tennisplatz oder im Fitness-Studio lädt das Spa zur Entspannung ein.

06 | 07 Not only the hotel's outstanding service but also the natural panorama give the guests an endless feeling of grandeur.

Nicht nur der überlegene Service des Hotels, sondern auch das Naturpanorama führt zu einem beständigen Gefühl von Erhabenheit.

casa casuarina | miami beach . florida
DESIGN: Eldin Freeman, Versace

Certainly a great contrast to the rest of the surroundings in the middle of the historic art deco quarter in Miami, this Italian-style villa is one of the remaining monuments to glamour, cultivation and fame. Each of its ten suites has its own unique décor that captures another element of the multifaceted, cosmopolitan spirit of the house with its artistic murals, fanciful frescos, doors and windows made of French stained-glass, as well as aesthetically-decorated marble halls. In addition to the butler service, guests are also provided with another extra service: according the hotel's information, their spa is not any ordinary body care station but a retreat from everyday stress. For the hotel's 75th anniversary, the owners of the Casa Casuarina gave themselves the gift of an exclusive club, in which one can become a member by invitation only. But do not worry—all the other guests are still welcome and may now take part in the exclusive atmosphere.

Diese italienisch anmutende Villa, die unvereinbar mit der Umgebung mitten im historischen Art déco-Viertel Miamis liegt, ist ein verbliebenes Monument des Glamours, von Kultiviertheit und Ruhm. Jede ihrer 10 Suiten hat ein eigenes, einzigartiges Dekor, das mit kunstvollen Wandmalereien, fantasiereichen Fresken, Türen und Fenstern aus französischem Buntglas sowie kunstvoll gestalteten Marmorfluren ein anderes Element des vielseitigen, weltoffenen Geistes des Hauses erfasst. Neben dem Butlerservice steht den Gästen noch ein weiteres Extra zur Verfügung: ein Spa, das laut Auskunft nicht nur eine alltägliche Körperpflegestation ist, sondern ein Refugium vor den Sorgen des Alltags. Zum 75-jährigen Bestehen des Hotels schenkten sich die Besitzer der Casa Casuarina einen exklusiven Club, in dem man nur nach Einladung Mitglied werden kann. Aber keine Angst – auch alle anderen Gäste sind gern weiterhin gesehen, und dürfen nun an der exklusiven Atmosphäre teilhaben.

01 | Ready for five o'clock tea? The reading corner in Casa Casuarina.

Fertig für den Fünfuhr-Tee? Leseecke im Casa Casuarina.

02 | The spa with its Oriental influences.

Spa mit orientalischen Einflüssen.

03 | Pre-Raphaelite murals remind us of the time of the great empires of the world. Even if the great empires have now vanished–their glory still lives on in the Casa Casuarina.

Präraffaelitische Wandmalereien erinnern an die Zeit der großen Weltimperien. Auch wenn die Imperien verschwunden sind – ihr Glanz lebt wenigstens in der Casa Casuarina weiter.

04 | The mosaics of the hotel pool would have been an honor even for a Roman manor-house.

Die Mosaiken des Hotelpools würden selbst einem römischen Herrenhaus zur Ehre gereichen.

01 | Bedroom in The Setai.

Schlafzimmer im The Setai.

the setai | miami beach . florida

DESIGN: Jaya Pratomo Ibrahim from Jaya & Associates, Jean Michel Gathy from Denniston International

Miami South Beach – a long-time synonym for summer, sun, beach, and art deco. The American hotel industry experienced the meaning of Asian hospitality with the opening of The Setai in 2005. The building on Collins Avenue was the original site of the Dempsey Vanderbilt Hotel in the 1930's. The Aman Resort hotelier, Adrian Zecha, along with a group of investment developers, has built the tallest building on the seemingly endless beaches of Miami. It sits upon a throne amid palm gardens with sparkling azure pools and directly at the edge of the white sand beach of the Atlantic Ocean. The Setai recreates the almost forgotten American glamour and style of days gone by and combines it with echoes of the art deco era of Shanghai. Even in the lobby made of teak and bronze, no doubt remains that the highest elegance and comfort also await guests in their rooms. The only disappointment is that champagne does not flow out of the taps. One is, however, quickly consoled because the each of the 75 rooms and 50 suites pays attention to the guests with their soft silhouettes, silk fabrics, and black granite bathrooms with bath accessories by Acqua di Parma. Zecha's sense for the highest personal service and privacy are also evident in the far-east inspired spa with the extraordinary spa suites and in the restaurant with its trans-ethnic cuisine.

Miami South Beach – das ist schon lange ein Synonym für Sommer, Sonne, Strand und Art déco. Mit Eröffnung des The Setai im Jahr 2005 erlebt die amerikanische Hotellerie aber auch, was asiatische Gastfreundschaft bedeutet. Das Gebäude an der Collins Avenue war in den 1930ern ursprünglich das Dempsey Vanderbilt Hotel. Dahinter hat der Amanresort Gründer Adrian Zecha mit einer Investorengruppe das höchste Gebäude am endlos erscheinenden Strand von Miami erbauen lassen. Es thront inmitten tropischer Palmengärten mit azurblauen Pools und ist direkt mit dem weißen Sandstrand am Atlantik verbunden. Zecha lässt im The Setai längst vergessen geglaubten amerikanischen Glanz und Glamour wiederaufleben und verbindet ihn mit Anklängen an die kunstvolle Art déco-Ära von Shanghai. Schon in der Lobby aus Teak und Bronze wird kein Zweifel daran gelassen, dass die Gäste auch in ihren Zimmern höchste Eleganz und Komfort erwarten wird. Die einzige Enttäuschung ist, dass kein Champagner aus den Wasserhähnen fließt. Schnell ist man jedoch darüber getröstet, denn die 75 Zimmer und 50 Suiten werben um die Gunst jedes Gastes mit weichen Silhouetten, hellen Stoffen und Granitbädern mit Accessoires von Acqua di Parma. Zechas Sinn für höchstpersönlichen Service und Privatsphäre zeigt sich auch im fernöstlich angehauchten Spa mit herrlichen Spa-Suiten und im Restaurant mit trans-ethnischer Küche.

02 03

04

02 | Atmosphere like in a lavish living room: The spa area of the Setai.

Atmosphäre wie in einem edlen Wohnzimmer: der Spabereich des Setai.

03 | In the anteroom of the spa area, the right program can be put together from a large selection of cosmetics.

Im Vorzimmer des Spabereichs kann aus einer großen Auswahl an Kosmetika das richtige Programm zusammengestellt werden.

04 | Coherent lines are created with color in all the rooms and suites and guarantees the subtle charm of the hotel.

Farblich werden in allen Zimmern und Suiten kohärente Linien geschaffen und der dezente Charakter des Hotels gewahrt.

05 | The pool makes playful use of the Asian elements and creates an impressive effect by candlelight.

Der Pool spielt mit asiatischen Elementen und setzt auf stimmungsvolle Effekte durch Kerzenlicht.

05

the standard miami | miami beach . florida

DESIGN: Shawn Hausman and André Balazs Properties, Alison Spear (project architect)

It is certainly not easy to be André Balazs. Every hotel that he designs is confronted with the highest of expectations, and sets new standards in design and architecture. The new Standard in Miami once again exceeds all expectations. The former Lido Spa Hotel was transformed into a quiet, exclusive, completely superlative spa. The marble walls, terrazzo floors and steel elevators were retained. Like as second design level, a Scandinavian sauna theme was added to the design. What is intriguing is that the two levels do not necessarily coordinate. The bold primary colors of a Swedish summer house are found everywhere, as well as the typical wooden beams of a Finnish sauna. The spa concentrates on all types of water therapy, most of which are public. The bathing complex is outdoors and is complete with a Jacuzzi, arctic plunges and waterfalls. A Turkish hamam, a Swedish sauna and an endless pool to relax the entire day. Miami's party scene lies in the distance because the hotel is located on Belle Isle. In complete concentration on his own relaxation, every guest can then re-formulate the standard definition of the word "heavenly".

Es ist bestimmt nicht einfach André Balazs zu sein. Jedes Hotel, das er entwirft, ist mit den allerhöchsten Erwartungen konfrontiert, und setzt neue Standards in Design und Architektur. Das neue Standard in Miami übertrifft nun noch einmal alle Erwartungen. Das ehemalige Lido Spa Hotel ist in ein ruhiges, exklusives, komplett Superlativ-Spa umgebaut worden. Die Marmorwände, Terrazzo-Böden und Stahlaufzüge wurden erhalten. Wie eine zweite Entwurfsebene wurde dem Design ein skandinavisches Sauna-Thema hinzugefügt. Dass die beiden Ebenen nicht unbedingt zusammenpassen, macht den Reiz aus. Die kräftigen Primärfarben eines schwedischen Sommerhauses sind überall zu finden, ebenso wie die typischen Holzlattenverschalungen einer finnischen Sauna. Das Spa konzentriert sich auf alle Formen von Wasserbehandlungen, die meisten davon sind öffentlich. Die Badeanlage im Freien ist mit Jacuzzi, Abkühlbecken und Wasserfall ausgestattet. Ein türkisches Hamam, eine schwedische Sauna und ein Endlos-Pool, um den ganzen Tag zu entspannen. Die Partyszene Miamis ist fern, denn das Hotel liegt auf Belle Isle. Und so kann jeder Gast in völliger Konzentration auf die eigene Entspannung seine Standarddefinition des Wortes „himmlisch" neu formulieren.

01 | Swedish summer house meets André Balasz' design: The Standard Miami.
Schwedisches Sommerhaus trifft auf André Balasz' Design: The Standard Miami.

02

02 | Far from Miami's party scene and you can have a wonderfully restful and relaxing sleep in the hotel's freshly made beds.

Fernab von der Partyszene Miamis und restlos entspannt schläft es sich wunderbar in den frisch bezogenen Hotelbetten.

03 | **04** In the spa, there are numerous types of water therapies to choose from, including a Swedish sauna and a Turkish hamam.

Im Spa stehen zahlreiche verschiedene Formen der Wasserbehandlung zur Auswahl, darunter findet sich eine schwedische Sauna und ein türkischer Hamam.

05 | The pool lies like a small oasis on the grounds of The Standard Miami, that is located on Belle Island, a hideaway for all those that find Miami too hectic.

Der Pool liegt wie eine eigene kleine Oase auf dem Gelände des The Standard Miami, das sich auf der Belle Isle befindet, einem Fluchtpunkt für alle, denen Miami zu hektisch wird.

03 04

mandarin oriental, miami | miami . florida

D E S I G N :   RTKL Associates, Hirsch Bedner & Associates, Tony Chi & Associates (restaurant design)

It is difficult to say which of the many hotels of the Mandarin Oriental Group is the most beautiful—it is easier to emphasize the specialties of each location, because service, elegance and comfort have attained the same high standards in all of the hotels. All 327 rooms and 31 suites of the Mandarin Oriental in Miami have a view of the Bay of Biscayne: many even offer a view of the skyline of Miami. The Bay of Biscayne is part of the Biscayne National Park that consists of a chain of islands whose tropical climate is home to many rare plants and animals. And even if these cannot be seen directly from the hotel, just the view of the bay from the restaurant is worth it, from there the guest can watch the ships passing through. The suites give a bit of the Asian attitude towards life. Bamboo floor and sliding walls covered with rice paper are based on traditional Japanese architecture. The rooms are designed according to the Feng Shui guidelines. The traditional philosophy behind Feng Shui, in which the spirits of the air and water should be appealed to and deals with observing the heavens and the earth, is realized in the Mandarin Oriental. Not only the waters of the Bay of Biscayne invite guests to observe them, but also the pool which is surrounded by palm trees.

Es ist schwer zu sagen, welches der vielen Hotels der Mandarin Oriental Gruppe das Schönste ist – leichter ist es, bei jedem einzelnen die Besonderheiten des Standorts hervorzuheben, denn Service, Eleganz und Komfort haben in allen Häusern einen gleich hohen Standard erreicht. Alle 327 Zimmer und 31 Suiten des Mandarin Oriental in Miami schauen auf die Biscayne-Bucht, viele bieten dazu noch einen Blick auf die Skyline von Miami. Die Biscayne Bucht ist Teil des Biscayne Nationalparks, der aus einer Reihe von Inseln besteht, deren tropisches Klima die Heimat von seltenen Tieren und Pflanzen ist. Und auch wenn diese vom Hotel nicht direkt zu sehen sind, so lohnt doch schon allein der Blick vom Restaurant aus auf die Bucht: von dort aus kann der Gast die durch die Bucht fahrenden Schiffe beobachten. Die Suiten lassen einen Hauch von asiatischem Lebensgefühl aufkommen. Bambusboden und mit Reispapier bezogene Schiebewände basieren auf traditioneller japanischer Architektur. Die Zimmer sind nach Feng Shui-Kriterien gestaltet. Die traditionelle Vorstellung von Feng Shui, in der man sich die Geister der Luft und des Wassers geneigt machen soll, und die davon handelt, den Himmel und die Erde zu beobachten, wird im Mandarin Oriental verwirklicht. Nicht nur das Meer in der Biscayne Bucht lädt zur Wasserbeobachtung ein, sondern auch der palmengesäumte Pool.

01 A harbinger of luxury: The hotel lobby
Ein Vorbote des Luxus: die Hotellobby

02 | Every individual room of the hotel clearly reiterates why the Mandarin Oriental has been become a trademark world wide: Asian understatement with perfect service.

Jeder einzelne Raum des Hotels macht ein weiteres Mal deutlich, warum das Mandarin Oriental weltweit zu einer Marke geworden ist – asiatisches Understatement bei perfektem Service.

03 | Could also pass for a museum: The Mandarin Oriental's art collection.

Könnte auch als ein Museum durchgehen: Objektsammlung des Mandarin Oriental.

04 | Twenty-four hour room service is one of the standards at the Mandarin Oriental, Miami–breakfast in bed can also be arranged upon request.

24 h Zimmerservice gehört zu einer der Selbstverständlichkeiten im Mandarin Oriental, Miami – auf Wunsch kann auch ein Frühstück im Bett arrangiert werden.

02 03
04

mandarin oriental, new york | new york . new york

DESIGN: Hirsch Bedner & Associates; Brennan Beer Gorman, Architects, L.L.P.; Tony Chi & Associates (restaurant design)

While the Mandarin Oriental in Miami offers a view of the waves of the Bay of Biscayne, its sister hotel in New York guarantees an extraordinary view of the streets of Manhattan. New York has always been a city open to all cultures and so the Asian heir to the hotel chain fits effortlessly in the prestigious Time Warner Center as well. It lies between the 35th and 54th floors in which the spectacular floor-to ceiling windows flood the rooms with lights of the metropolis. The guest will find a mix of modern furnishings, art deco style furniture and elegant, Asian-inspired design in the 248 luxurious rooms and suites. Richly decorated kimonos adorn the walls. Especially eye-catching is the contemporary art, among the highlights are two glass sculptures by Dale Chihuly. In addition to the feasts for the eyes, let us not forget the guests' palate: the hotel's own restaurant offers Asian cuisine that was even worthy of a prize awarded by the professional gourmets of the Michelin Restaurant Guide. And in order to make the experience perfect—while dining, guests can also enjoy the design of the restaurant that was created by the designer, Tony Chi. A visit to the MOBar is recommended before going out to join the nightlife. It is also located on the grounds.

Während das Mandarin Oriental Miami einen Blick auf die Wellen der Biscayne Bucht bietet, gewährt das Schwesterhotel in New York eine überwältigende Aussicht auf die Straßenschluchten Manhattans. Schon immer war New York eine für alle Kulturen offene Stadt, und so fügt sich auch das asiatische Erbe der Hotelkette mühelos in das prestigeträchtige Time Warner Center ein. Dort liegt es zwischen der 35. und 54. Etage, in der die raumhohen Fenster die Räume mit dem Licht der Metropole fluten. In den 248 luxuriösen Zimmern und Suiten findet der Gast einen Mix aus moderner Einrichtung, Möbeln im Art déco-Stil und elegantem, asiatisch inspiriertem Design. Verzierte Kimonos schmücken die Wände. Ein besonderer Blickfang ist die zeitgenössische Kunst; zu den Highlights gehören zwei Glasskulpturen von Dale Chihuly. Neben dem Augenschmaus kommt aber auch die feine Zunge der Gäste nicht zu kurz: Das hauseigene Restaurant Asiate bietet asiatische Küche an, die sogar den Berufsgourmets des Michelin Führers einen Preis wert war. Und um das Erlebnis perfekt zu machen, können sich die Gäste während des Essens auch noch an der Gestaltung des Restaurants erfreuen, die der Designer Tony Chi geschaffen hat. Bevor man sich dann ins Nachtleben stürzt, ist ein Besuch in der MOBar empfehlenswert, die sich ebenfalls im unteren Geschoss befindet.

01 | Relaxed high above the streets of Manhattan in the Mandarin Oriental New York.

Im Mandarin Oriental New York entspannt hoch über den Straßen Manhattans.

02

01 | The former colonial style of the entire hotel complex is also evident even at the hotel pool.

Auch am Hotelpool ist der zurückgenommen koloniale Stil der gesamten Anlage spürbar.

02 | Even the halls of the hotel are so impeccably designed that guests feel just as at home in them as they do in their rooms.

Selbst die Hotelflure sind so sorgfältig gestaltet, dass man sich in ihnen ebenso gern aufhält wie in seinem Zimmer.

03 | Bedroom in the Four Seasons Resort Great Exuma.

Schlafzimmer im Four Seasons Resort Great Exuma.

04 | The spa offers skin-cooling earth and clay rituals.

Das Spa bietet hautkühlende Erd- und Lehmrituale an.

05 | The room's balconies have a view of the ocean but they offer more shade and are closer to the guest's suite as well as the room service available there.

Die Balkone der Zimmer zeigen auf den Strand, bieten aber mehr Schatten und größere Nähe zur eigenen Suite und dem dort erhältlichen Zimmerservice.

one&only ocean club | paradise island . bahamas

DESIGN: Hill Glazier Architects, Barry Design Associates, Perdian International

One would almost think that this is a Mediterranean complex: The One&Only Ocean Club consists of different buildings spread out over a hillary park including three colonial Bahamian style villas. Hibiscus and bougainvillea bushes line the way from the beach to the terrace garden. One almost feels like the "Roi Soleil" because the gardens are fashioned after the gardens in Versailles and decorated with bronze and marble statues. At the highest point, there are impressive archways from the ruins of an Augustinian cloister from the 12th century. Guests may stroll here and be inspired by the contemplative aura of the historical building. The One&Only Ocean Club understands how to create a balance between lightness and heaviness. All of the areas are bright and open; the rooms, however, have beds made of dark, heavy mahogany. The light fabrics separate this so that no one must fall into melancholy. Even the cuisine of the hotel restaurant is focused on balance. On the terrace, located on the crest of a dune, serves well-balanced gourmet cuisine.

Fast glaubt man sich an einem mediterranen Ort zu befinden: Der One&Only Ocean Club besteht aus verschiedenen, auf eine hügelige Landschaft verteilten Gebäuden, inklusive drei im Kolonialstil der Bahamas erbauten Villen. Hibiskus- und Bougainvilleasträucher säumen den Weg vom Strand hinauf zum Terrassengarten. Dort kann man sich ganz wie ein Sonnenkönig fühlen, denn der Garten ist nach dem Vorbild von Versailles angelegt und mit europäischen Bronze- und Marmorstatuen dekoriert. An der höchsten Stelle erheben sich die beeindruckenden Bögen der Ruine eines Augustinerklosters aus dem 12. Jahrhundert. Hier können die Gäste umherstreifen und sich von der kontemplativen Ausstrahlung der alten Mauern inspirieren lassen. Der One&Only Ocean Club versteht es, eine Balance zwischen Leichtigkeit und Schwere herzustellen. Alle Räume sind hell und offen, die Zimmer verfügen jedoch über Betten aus schwerem, dunklem Mahagoniholz. Die hellen Stoffe brechen dies jedoch wieder auf, so dass niemand in Schwermut verfallen muss. Auch die Küche des hauseigenen Restaurants ist ganz auf Balance ausgerichtet. Auf der Terrasse, die sich auf dem Kamm einer Düne befindet, wird ausgewogene Gourmetküche serviert.

01 | One of the bedrooms in the three villas of the One&Only Ocean Club.

Eines der Schlafzimmer der drei Villen des One&Only Ocean Clubs.

02 | Influences from the Balinese culture are not only noticeable in the architecture but also in the interaction with the guests: In the One&Only Ocean Club, friendly service is definitive.

Einflüsse der balinesischen Kultur sind nicht nur in der Architektur, sondern auch im Umgang mit den Gästen zu bemerken: Freundlichkeit bestimmt das Leben im One&Only Ocean Club.

02

03 | The entire hotel complex as well as the hotel pool is surrounded by greenery that not only gives shade, but also delicate fragrance.

Der Hotelpool ist ebenso wie der gesamte Club mit blühenden Sträuchern begrünt, die nicht nur Schatten, sondern auch Duft spenden.

01 | Lounge atmosphere in the Amanyara.
Lounge Atmosphäre im Amanyara.

amanyara | providenciales . turks and caicos islands
DESIGN: Team around Jean Michel Gathy

The Providenciales Island in the Atlantic Ocean belongs to the Turks and Caicos Islands of the British West Indies. Turquoise-colored water, long, white sand beaches, pristine nature and the famous colorful coral reef of the Marine National Park make this island a very promising place to take a vacation. Amanyara lies on the northwestern-most peak of the island, borders on this reef and demonstrates the promise held in its name: "Aman" stands for peace in Sanskrit, "yara" means more or less "place" in the language of the indigenous people, the Arawaks. A peaceful place that is reflected in its fascinating architecture. There are 40 guest pavilions, some are nestled in an adjoining lake landscape, others are directly on the beach that are connected by a spacious terrace construction and are gently snuggled into the coast with their natural construction style. Bright sun decks, a swimming pool and many lounge-like niches invite the guests stay a while a relax. The relaxing spa treatments are the perfect complement, upon request they can also be carried out in the guest pavilions. For the athletic aspects, there are also the tennis courts with flood light system as well as the variety of beach and water sports, from sailing to complete diving equipment. Diving courses for every level of skill are offered by the hotel diving club and offers all the diving-enthusiastic visitors a fascinating look into a yet untouched underwater world.

Die Insel Providenciales im atlantischen Ozean gehört zu den Turks und Caicos Inseln Britisch Westindiens. Türkisfarbenes Meer, lange, weiße Sandstrände, unberührte Natur und das berühmte farbenprächtige Korallenriff des Marine National Parks machen diese Inseln zu einem wunderbaren Urlaubsversprechen. Amanyara am nordwestlichsten Zipfel der Insel gelegen, grenzt an dieses Riff an und führt das Versprechen im Namen fort: "Aman" steht im Sanskrit für Frieden, "yara" bedeutet in der Sprache der Ureinwohner, die Arawaks, so viel wie "Platz". Ein friedvoller Platz, der sich in einer faszinierenden Architektur widerspiegelt. 40 Gästepavillons, manche darunter eingebettet in eine angelegte Seenlandschaft, andere direkt am Strand gelegen, sind durch eine großzügige Terrassenlandschaft verbunden und schmiegen sich in ihrer natürlichen Bauweise behutsam an die Küste an. Lichtdurchflutete Sonnendecks, ein Swimming-Pool sowie die vielen loungigen Ecken laden dabei zum Verweilen ein. Passend dazu gibt es erholsame Spa-Anwendungen, auf Wunsch in der privaten Sphäre der Gästepavillons. Für das sportliche Pendant sorgen Tennisplätze mit Flutlichtanlage sowie das reiche Angebot an Strand- und Wassersportmöglichkeiten, über Segelboote bis hin zur kompletten Tauchausrüstung. Tauchkurse für jeden Level bietet der hoteleigene Tauch-Club, so erschließt sich allen tauchbegeisterten Besuchern der faszinierende Blick in eine noch unberührte Unterwasserwelt.

02 | A loose translation of Amanyara means: „peaceful place". The carefully and attentively furnished suites with are an honor to its name.

Amanyara bedeutet übersetzt in etwa: „friedlicher Platz". Die mit Sorgfalt ausgestatteten Suiten machen diesem Namen alle Ehre.

03 | The hotel sun deck has a marvelous view of the vastness of the ocean. Guests will still dream of the peacefulness of this place long after the vacation is over.

Das Sonnendeck des Hotels gibt den Blick auf die Weite des Ozeans frei. Noch lange nach dem Aufenthalt träumen die Gäste von der Ruhe dieses Ortes.

cap juluca | maunday's bay . anguilla

DESIGN: Oskar Farmer, Bob Perkins, Xanadu

The lonely island on the northern edge of the Antilles is approximately 16 miles long and approximately three miles wide. It has neither the rain forests nor the rocky coasts of the other Caribbean islands. Anguilla is formed by a lovely, lush-green hilly landscape dotted with sparse settlements. Juluca is located here, around 15 minutes away from the small airport, Wallblake, at the southwestern end of the island. The villas of the resort are like a row of pearls on the white, crescent beach. Almost everything can be rented there, from the superior rooms that have over 2.150 square feet on the ground floors, to the luxury rooms or junior suites or the one-bedroom suites on the first floor with ocean-view terraces, to a complete villa with its own pool and three to five bedrooms. The spa landscape, that started business in mid-2003 and is built on the headland between the two bays, is the undisputed highlight of the hotel. Holistic, preventative medicine is on the program, including yoga. Transformation therapies and astrological consultation (even for those who do not believe in it at all). The casual, always friendly and never servile attitude of the staff is especially refreshing. Together with its unique setting, it is the comprehensive and yet completely informal atmosphere that make Cap Juluca an appealing first class resort.

Das ruhige Eiland am Nordrand der Antillen ist gerade einmal 25 Kilometer lang und rund fünf Kilometer breit. Es gibt weder üppige Regenwälder noch die hohen, steilen Felsküsten anderer Karibikinseln. Anguilla prägt eine liebliche, sattgrüne Hügellandschaft mit verstreuten Ansiedlungen. Hier liegt Juluca, rund 15 Minuten vom Kleinflughafen Wallblake entfernt am südwestlichen Ende der Insel. Wie Perlen sind die Villen des Resorts entlang des weißen, mondsichelförmigen Strands aufgereiht. Zu mieten gibt es so ziemlich alles, vom knapp 200 Quadratmeter großen Superior Room in den Erdgeschossen, über die im ersten Obergeschoss befindlichen Luxury Rooms beziehungsweise Junior- oder One Bedroom-Suiten mit Meerblick-Terrassen bis hin zu kompletten Villen mit eigenem Pool und drei bis fünf Schlafzimmern. Die Spa-Landschaft, die auf der Landzunge zwischen den beiden Buchten Mitte 2003 ihren Betrieb aufgenommen hat, ist das unbestrittene Highlight des Hotels. Auf dem Programm stehen ganzheitliche Präventivmedizin, inklusive Yoga, Transformationstherapien und astrologische Beratung (auch für die, die eigentlich überhaupt nicht an so was glauben). Wohltuend ist ganz besonders die immer nette, lockere und nie unterwürfige Art des Personals. Zusammen mit dem einzigartigen Setting ist es das umfangreiche und gleichzeitig vollkommen zwanglose Angebot, das Cap Juluca zum sympathischen Erste-Klasse Resort macht.

01 | Just like in 1001 Arabian Nights: The Juluca in Maunday's Bay.

Wie in 1001 Nacht: Das Juluca in Maunday's Bay.

02 | Especially suited to re-read "Ali Baba and the 40 Thieves": The cozy furnishings of the Juluca.

Besonders geeignet um mal wieder Ali Baba und die 40 Räuber zu lesen: die gemütliche Einrichtung des Juluca.

03 | The bathrooms with high-quality furnishings are found in all the suites of the hotels, even in those that are less expensive.

Hochwertig eingerichtete Badezimmer finden sich in allen Suiten des Hotels, auch in denen, für die man weniger tief in die Tasche greifen muss.

04 | There is nothing that will take your mind off your comfort in the Juluca. The hotel intentionally left out the kitschy oriental-style.

Im Juluca lenkt nichts vom eigenen Wohlbefinden ab. Auf kitschige Orientalistik hat man hier verzichtet.

05 | In Maunday's Bay, as well as on all the small islands, guests have the advantage of never being further than a hop, skip and a jump from the beach.

Wie auf allen kleinen Inseln hat man auch am Maunday's Bay den Vorteil, nie weiter als einen Katzensprung vom Strand entfernt zu sein.

06 | After an astrological consultation in the spa, guests can reflect on what they have just learned at the hotel pool.

Nach der astrologischen Beratung im Spa kann man am Hotelpool über das eben Erfahrene nachdenken.

02   03

04 05
06

carlisle bay | antigua . british west indies

DESIGN: Mary Fox Linton, Gordon Campbell Gray

This resort on a hidden beach before the rain forests and rolling hills purposefully left out the colonial facades. Instead the pleasantly cool interior design attracts one's attention to the bright colors of the exotic flower gardens and the foaming Caribbean sea—at least when one is not too busy strolling through the 786 to 1.610 square feet of the suites. Guest feel rejuvenated after a visit to the BLUE Spa when they have enjoyed the spa's private sun deck on an Asian day bed. The city life can be completely forgotten in the Carlisle, without having to do without life's little pleasantries. In every room there is an espresso machine that allows guests to prepare a wonderful cappuccino within their own four walls, that in contrast to all the "to go" drinks can be enjoyed in peace. For example, in the hotel library that Tatler described as "the funkiest library on earth". In the Carlisle, it is emphasized that one does not miss out on intellectual entertainment. The hotel has its own cinema that shows films every evening and has over 45 seats. There is even something for the young ones: children's films are shown during the day.

Dieses Resort an einem versteckten Strand vor Regenwäldern und sanften Hügeln verzichtet ganz bewusst auf koloniale Versatzstücke. Stattdessen lenkt das angenehm unterkühlte Design der Innenräume die gesamte Aufmerksamkeit auf die leuchtenden Farben der exotischen Blumengärten und die schäumende See – zumindest wenn man nicht zu sehr beschäftigt ist, die 73 bis 150 Quadratmeter der Suiten zu erkunden. Die Gäste dürfen sich nach dem Besuch des BLUE Spa verjüngt fühlen, wenn sie das eigene Sonnendeck auf einem asiatischen Tagesbett genießen. Das Stadtleben kann im Carlisle ganz und gar vergessen werden, ohne dass auf die kleinen Extras, die das Leben schön machen, verzichtet werden muss. In jedem Zimmer befindet sich eine Espressomaschine, die es den Gästen erlaubt, sich in den eigenen vier Wänden einen herrlichen Cappuccino zuzubereiten, der aber im Gegensatz zu den weit verbreiteten To-go-Getränken in Ruhe getrunken werden kann. Zum Beispiel in der Bibliothek des Hauses, die von Tatler als „funkiest library on earth" bezeichnet wurde. Überhaupt legt man im Carlisle Bay Wert darauf, dass auch die intellektuelle Unterhaltung nicht zu kurz kommt. Im hauseigenen Kino, das über 45 Plätze verfügt, werden jeden Abend Filme gezeigt, selbst für die jüngsten ist immer etwas dabei: tagsüber flimmern auch Kinderfilme über die Leinwand.

01 | In Carlisle Bay simplicity is emphasized instead of colonial facades.
In Carlisle Bay setzt man auf Schlichtheit statt auf koloniale Anleihen.

03

02 | 03 The spacious suites are meticulously furnished and give off the same lightness as the entire complex. The feeling of floating high above things is intensified by the rooms that are open on almost all sides.

Die geräumigen Suiten sind sorgfältig eingerichtet und verströmen doch dieselbe Leichtigkeit wie das gesamte Anwesen. Durch die nach beinahe allen Seiten offenen Räume wird das Gefühl eines Schwebens über den Dingen noch verstärkt.

04 | The restaurant serves a light fare that is adapted to the climate – and as
with all the furnishings – uses bold accents from all kinds of cultures.

Das Restaurant serviert dem Klima angemessene, leichte Küche und setzt
– wie auch bei der Einrichtung – auf kräftige Akzente aus allerlei Kulturen.

05 | The hotel's public spaces are almost as quiet as in a cloister. Yet there is no need to abstain from pleasure at the Carlisle.

Die öffentlichen Bereiche des Hotels sind beinahe so ruhig wie der Kreuzgang in einem Kloster. Allerdings muss man im Carlisle nicht auf den Genuss verzichten.

05

le sereno | st. barthélemy . french west indies
DESIGN: Christian Liaigre

Le Sereno, they understand that too much input can be distracting and disturbing when you just want to find yourself and regenerate after a long and stressful period at work. This hotel with its 37 exquisitely furnished suites is one of the especially intimate and elegant gems of the Caribbean. It lies directly on an approximately 656 feet long beach in the picturesque, turquoise-colored Grand-Cul-de-Sac Bay. The famous Parisian interior designer, Christian Liaigre, is responsible for the design of the elegant suites with their minimalist furniture in gray and creme. Immediately upon entering the hotel with its clear lines, white fabrics, warm woods, it invokes the relaxed feeling that is typical for St. Barthélemy: hotel service includes a private chauffeur service to the airport, 24-hour room service, a gourmet restaurant and a boutique. In the last few years, the island of St. Barthélemy has been developing into an important center of Caribbean cuisine. Beside the hotel restaurant in Le Sereno, over 80 other restaurants offer their light delicacies so it is recommended that every guest go on a "cuisine safari" for a change.

Im Le Sereno hat man verstanden, dass allzu viel Spielerei störend und ablenkend sein kann, wenn man einfach nur mit sich selbst zusammen sein will, um sich nach langer und stressiger Arbeitszeit zu regenerieren. Mit nur 37 exquisit möblierten Suiten gehört dieses Hotel zu den besonders intimen und eleganten Schmuckstücken der Karibik. Es liegt direkt an einem etwa 200 Meter langen Strand in der pittoresken, türkisfarbenen Grand-Cul-de-Sac-Bucht. Der bekannte Pariser Innenarchitekt Christian Liaigre ist für das Design der eleganten Suiten mit ihren minimalistischen Möbeln in Grau und Creme verantwortlich. Gerade Linien, weiße Stoffe und dunkle, warme Hölzer lösen schon beim Betreten das entspannte Gefühl aus, das typisch für St. Barthélemy ist: Der Hotelservice stellt privaten Fahrdienst zum Flughafen, 24 Stunden Zimmerservice, ein Gourmetrestaurant und eine Boutique zur Verfügung. Überhaupt hat sich in den letzten Jahren die Insel St. Barthélemy zu einer Hochburg der karibischen Küche entwickelt. Neben dem Le Sereno bieten noch 80 weitere Restaurants ihre leichten Köstlichkeiten an, so dass zur Abwechslung auch eine Gaumensafari jedem Gast auf der Insel zu empfehlen ist.

01 | Little is required in order to be happy.
Froh zu sein bedarf es wenig.

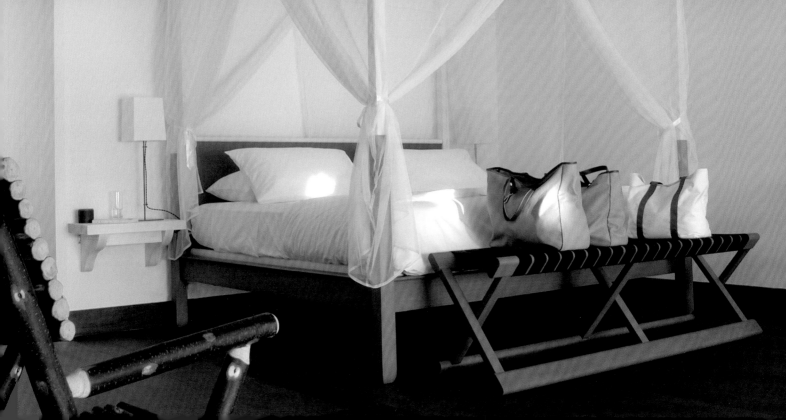

02 | Only the fishermen are closer to the sea when dining at the restaurant in the Le Sereno.

Beim Essen dem Meer noch näher zu sein als im Restaurant des Le Sereno gelingt wohl nur Fischern.

03 | Bedroom.

Schlafzimmer.

04 | When the guests have returned home, they can have their vacation pictures turned into photo wallpaper.

Sobald die Gäste des Le Sereno nach Hause zurückgekehrt sind, können sie sich ihre Urlaubsfotos zu einer Fototapete umarbeiten lassen.

05 | Especially at night, the way to the gourmet restaurant itself is pure pleasure and inspires guests to take a long stroll after the evening meal on the way back to their rooms.

Vor allem bei Nacht ist schon allein der Weg zum Gourmetrestaurant das reinste Vergnügen, und animiert nach dem Essen zu einem ausgedehnten Verdauungsspaziergang auf dem Weg zurück ins Zimmer.

01 | The House is a paradise for elegant romantics and those who would like to be.

The House ist ein Paradies für elegante Romantiker, und solche, die es gern werden möchten.

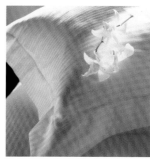

the house | barbados . british west indies
DESIGN: Luciano Colombo

A wooden bridge leads over the lake that is covered by blooming lilies. The idyllic island atmosphere receives new arrivals almost silently. Welcome to Barbados. The House that is anything other than just a house is also as unobtrusive as the first impression that visitors get. The luxury hotel that was opened in 2001 is the latest project of the Elegant Hotels Group located in Great Britain. The predominant color of the hotel is white—the interior, the walls, even the staff's clothing. A design that is intentionally subdued and entrusts itself to the charm of the surroundings. You can also have breakfast brought right to your bed, a special menu called "flavor to awaken your senses". Or you can begin the day with a fruit cocktail at the pool that is protected by anti-paparazzi shades. The quiet is only disturbed by the cheeky insects buzzing around. You can relax by taking a stroll on the private beach on which the hotel is located. The Beach Service offers cool drinks and chilled fruit. Guests also have other options available: sailing and windsurfing, of course, snorkeling and kayaking. Or a visit to Daphne's Restaurant located nearby. The establishment is a branch of the legendary London gourmet temple, Daphne's of Chelsea. On the menu: vegetarian dishes and Italian cuisine—from spaghetti al pesto to mussels with chickpeas.

Blühende Lilien bedecken den See, über den eine Holzbrücke führt. Leise, fast lautlos empfängt die Inselidylle Neuankömmlinge. Willkommen auf Barbados. So unaufdringlich wie der erste Eindruck, den Besucher gewinnen, gibt sich auch The House, das allerdings alles andere ist als nur ein Haus. Bei dem Luxushotel, 2001 eröffnet, handelt es sich um das jüngste Projekt der in Großbritannien beheimateten Elegant Hotels Group. Die vorherrschende Farbe des Hotels ist Weiß – das Interieur, die Wände, sogar die Kleidung der Hotelangestellten. Ein Design, das sich bewusst zurücknimmt und auf den Charme der Umgebung vertraut. Wer mag, lässt sich das Frühstück ans Bett bringen, ein spezielles Menü „Flavour to Awaken your Senses". Oder man beginnt den Tag, geschützt von Anti-Paparazzi-Schirmen, mit einem Fruchtcocktail am Pool. Die Ruhe stört allenfalls das Summen vorwitziger Insekten. Entspannung findet man bei einem Spaziergang am Privatstrand, an dem das House liegt. Ein Beach Service sorgt für kühle Getränke und offeriert eisgekühltes Obst. Darüber hinaus stehen den Gästen die Angebote der anderen Elegant Hotels offen: Segeln und Windsurfen, Schnorcheln natürlich, auch Kajak fahren. Oder ein Besuch im nahegelegenen Restaurant Daphne's. Das Lokal ist ein Ableger des berühmten Londoner Gourmet-Tempels Daphne's of Chelsea. Auf der Speisekarte: vegetarische Gerichte und italienische Cuisine – von Spaghetti al Pesto bis zu Muscheln mit Kichererbsen.

02 | Should you be able to avert your eyes from the beauty of the Caribbean, although it is unlikely, there are still many other sights to behold.

Falls man seinen Blick wider Erwarten doch einmal von den Schönheiten der Karibik ablenken kann, steht genügend andere Zerstreuung bereit.

03 | The most difficult decision that the guests have to make: hotel pool or beach?

Die schwierigste Entscheidung, die Gäste des House treffen müssen: Hotelpool oder Strand?

ikal del mar | playa del carmen . mexico

DESIGN: Ramiro Alatorre

There is unbroken optimism along the mostly 4-lane highway from Cancun to Tulum on the Riviera Maya. In the middle of this stretch of coast between Cancun and Playa del Carmen that is clearly created for mass tourism there is still enough room for a hidden luxury paradise. One of these is Ikal del Mar which means "poetry of the sea". Narrow paths wind between the ferns, bananas, cacti, tropical trees and shrubs to the 30 spacious bohios (bungalows). The layout of the rooms is exceptional. The living and sleeping areas are dominant with their dark tropical wooden floors and low-key, necessary furnishings, among other things, with a dining table for two people, rattan couch, basket chairs and media cabinet. The large glazed windows create a connection to nature, all with shady blinds as well as the two sliding doors on the veranda. One is made of glass and the other, for fresh air fans, has a screen that seamlessly connects the living room with the covered terrace and the in-ground plunge pool. Two round building cleverly fitting into each other house the sauna, steam bath, and a whirlpool illuminated by candlelight as well as the treatment rooms for massage and cosmetics. A special treat is the couples massage where both partners can experience a massage at the same time, two pallets on a stone platform surrounded by the jungle are covered by a fine mosquito screen.

Entlang der inzwischen größtenteils vierspurig ausgebauten Schnellstraße von Cancun nach Tulum an der mexikanischen Maya Rivieria herrscht ungebrochener Optimismus. Inmitten dieses sichtbar für Massentourismus angelegten Küstenabschnitts zwischen Cancun und Playa del Carmen ist trotzdem genügend Platz für versteckte Luxusparadiese erhalten geblieben. Eines davon ist das Ikal del Mar, auf Spanisch „Gedicht des Meeres". Zwischen Farnen, Bananen, Kakteen, tropischen Räumen und Büschen schlängeln sich die schmalen Pfade zu den 30 geräumigen Bohios (Bungalows). Gut gelungen ist die Raumeinteilung. Dominant ist der Wohn- und Schlafraum mit dunklen Tropenholzdielen und zurückhaltender, brauchbarer Möblierung, u.a. mit Esstisch für zwei Personen, Rattancouch, Korbsessel und Medienschrank. Verbindung mit der Natur schaffen die großflächigen Verglasungen, allesamt mit Schatten spendenden Lamellenläden ausgestattet sowie die beiden Veranda-Schiebetüren. Die einmal aus Glas und für Frischluftfanatiker nur mit Fliegengittern versehenen Türen verbinden nahtlos den Wohnraum mit der überdachten Terrasse und dem dort eingelassenen Erfrischungspool. Zwei geschickt ineinander verwobene Rundgebäude beherbergen Sauna, Dampfbad, einen mit Kerzen illuminierten Whirlpool sowie Behandlungsräume für Massage und Kosmetik. Besondere Aufmerksamkeit verdient die Paarmassage. Zwei Liegen auf einer von Dschungel umgebenen Steinplattform hinter dem Gebäude sind mit feinem Moskitonetz umhüllt.

01 | This is the way a child would paint paradise: The Ikal del Mar in the evening.

So würde ein Kind das Paradies malen: das Ikal del Mar am Abend

04 | 05

02 | 03 The hotel pool fits into the nature of the surrounds and makes you
feel as if you were swimming in a small lagoon.

Der Hotelpool ist in die Natur der Umgebung eingepasst, und lässt das
Gefühl aufkommen, eigentlich in einer kleinen Lagune zu schwimmen.

04 | 05 All the villas were erected with wood and stone from the region.

Alle Villen wurden mit Holz und Stein aus der Region errichtet.

06 | The ideal climate of the area surrounding Cancun not only makes the plants grow but also is favorable for the open construction style of the Ikal del Mar.

Das ideale Klima in der Umgebung Cancuns bringt nicht nur eine außergewöhnliche Pflanzenwelt zum Wachsen, sondern begünstigt auch die offene Bauweise des Ikal del Mar.

07 | Besides the oversized bed, guests also have comfortable chairs and a couch–an ideal place to relax.

Neben dem riesigen Bett stehen den Gästen gemütliche Sessel und eine Couch zur Verfügung - ein optimaler Rückzugsort.

esencia | riviera maya . mexico

DESIGN: Prohotel International, Alfonso Nuñez

Light and air are the central elements of a perfect vacation. Both are more than abundant in this hotel. After all, it seems as if the entire design concept is harmonized around it. Numerous, large sun terraces are grouped around the three-story hotel building, the former villa of an Italian royal family. In the open hallways with their bricked archways and the spacious entrance area make it sometimes hard to decide whether the guest is on the inside or the outside—without the guest feeling lost. It the lightness with which the complex seems to go its way that make time and space secondary categories. White is the dominant color in the nine rooms and ten garden suites. Thus the furnishings seem discreetly elegant without appearing minimal and cold. The almost black wooden furniture and accessories as well as strategically-placed colorful elements, for example blankets or tropical fruits, provide the Mexican accent. You can pick these fruits yourself while strolling across the over 20 hectare compound. Those who like to spend their vacation at the beach with family and friends, the Esencia hotel offers a villa with its own swimming pool. It is only a few steps to untouched beaches. The beach that is over three kilometers long is the starting point for leisure activities such as fishing or diving as well as trips with a sailboat.

Licht und Luft sind die zentralen Elemente eines perfekten Urlaubs. Beides gibt es in diesem Hotel im Überfluss. Schließlich scheint das gesamte Designkonzept darauf abgestimmt. Zahlreiche große Sonnenterrassen gruppieren sich um das drei Stockwerke hohe Hauptgebäude, die ehemalige Villa einer italienischen Adelsfamilie. Die offenen Gänge mit gemauerten Bögen und dem großzügigen Eingangsbereich machen es manchmal schwer zu bestimmen, ob man sich innen oder außen befindet ohne dass sich die Gäste verloren fühlen. Es ist die Leichtigkeit mit der in der Anlage alles seinen Weg zu gehen scheint, die Zeit und Raum zu nebensächlichen Kategorien werden lässt. Weiß ist die dominierende Farbe in den neun Zimmern und den zehn Garten-Suiten. So wirkt die Ausstattung zurückhaltend elegant, ohne minimalistisch kühl zu erscheinen. Für mexikanische Akzente sorgen dunkle, fast schwarze Holzmöbel und Accessoires sowie gezielt platzierte farbige Elemente, wie Tagesdecken oder tropische Früchte. Diese kann man bei einem Spaziergang über das 20 Hektar große Gelände auch selbst pflücken. Wer den Strandurlaub am liebsten mit Freunden oder der ganzen Familie verbringt, dem bietet das Esencia eigene Villen mit privatem Pool. Zum unberührten Meeresufer sind es nur wenige Schritte. Der über drei Kilometer lange Strand ist auch Ausgangspunkt für Freizeitaktivitäten, von Angel- und Tauchausflügen bis hin zu Touren mit dem Segelschiff.

01 | Sleeping quarters in one of the suites of the Esencia.

Schlafbereich in einer der Suiten des Esencia.

02 | The influence of the Italian nobility who once owned the Esencia is still visible today. Details such as the elaborate floor are still cherished and cared for.

Der Einfluss der italienischen Adelsfamilie, die einst das Esencia besaß, ist immer noch sichtbar. Details wie der aufwändige Fußboden werden in Ehren gehalten und gepflegt.

04

05

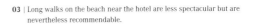

03 | Long walks on the beach near the hotel are less spectacular but are nevertheless recommendable.

Eine unspektakuläre aber dennoch empfehlenswerte Attraktion sind lange Strandspaziergänge in der Nähe des Hotels.

04 | The bar, in which you can have a cocktail after the first few laps, is located in direct proximity to the pool.

In unmittelbarer Nähe zum Pool befindet sich die Bar, in der man nach ein paar Bahnen die ersten Cocktails trinken kann.

05 | Dark offset pieces of the furnishings prevent the dominant white of the walls from creating a sterile atmosphere.

Dunkel abgesetzte Teile der Einrichtung verhindern, dass das dominierende Weiß der Wände eine sterile Atmosphäre erzeugt.

01 | The Resort has a view of one of the most beautiful beaches in Mexico.

Das Resort zeigt auf einen der schönsten Strände Mexikos.

las ventanas al paraíso, a rosewood resort | los cabos . mexico
DESIGN: Wilson & Associates Dallas, TX and Art Consultant Joan Warren Grady

Those who enter this hotel try their best during their stay not to leave it anymore. It not only offers an infinity pool, access to a sandy beach, and many recreational activities, but also outdoor yoga courses and aroma massages. The fireplace, marble showers and whirlpool create a relaxed atmosphere in the 71 suites. During the day, the secluded terraces in the ocean suites invite guests to a little refreshment in the private whirlpool. At night, they are an excellent location to observe the night sky with a telescope. Not only hobby astronomers, but also gourmets will be enthusiastic: besides the restaurant, the Sea Grill serves fresh delicacies from the sea. Guests can have a nightcap in the bar that has a selection of the best tequilas. For those who would like to enjoy all this in a more intimate atmosphere, room service is also available. Las Ventanas is probably one of the most wonderful places to propose as well—guests simply must return to celebrate their wedding too. The hotel is specialized in smaller wedding parties for up to 60 persons.

Wer dieses Hotel betritt, ist versucht es während des ganzen Aufenthalts nicht mehr zu verlassen. Es bietet nicht nur einen randlosen Pool, Zugang zum Sandstrand und viele Sportmöglichkeiten, sondern auch Yogakurse und Aromamassagen unter freiem Himmel. In den 71 Suiten schaffen Kaminfeuer, Marmorduschen und Whirlpool eine entspannte Atmosphäre. Nicht einsehbare Terrassen in den Strand-Suiten laden tagsüber zu einer Abkühlung im privaten Whirlpool ein, während sich nachts mit einem Teleskop der Sternenhimmel beobachten lässt. Nicht nur Hobbyastronomen, sondern auch Gourmets kommen auf ihre Kosten: neben dem Restaurant serviert ein Grill frische Köstlichkeiten aus dem Meer. Ein Absacker kann in der Bar eingenommen werden, die über eine Auswahl der besten Tequlias verfügt. Wer all das in etwas intimer Atmosphäre genießen möchte, kann den Zimmerservice nutzen. In dieser Atmosphäre einen Heiratsantrag zu machen, bietet sich besonders an – zum Heiraten sollte man nämlich unbedingt ins Las Ventanas zurückkehren. Für kleinere Hochzeitsgesellschaften bis zu 60 Personen ist man hier bestens ausgerüstet.

02   03

02 | Bedroom in the Las Ventanas al Paraíso, A Rosewood Resort.

Schlafzimmer im Las Ventanas al Paraíso, A Rosewood Resort.

03 | Three good reasons to visit this resort: the sea, the sea and the sea. What luck that the pool is directly adjacent to the water then it is not such a long way.

Drei gute Gründe, um das Resort zu besuchen: das Meer, das Meer und das Meer. Ein Glück, dass der Pool direkt an das Wasser angrenzt, dann hat man es nicht so weit.

04 | Small oases and the special kind of light in Los Cabos create a unique atmosphere.

Kleine Wasserstellen und das besondere Licht in Los Cabos erzeugen eine einzigartige Stimmung.

hotelito desconocido | puerto vallarta . mexico
DESIGN: Marcello Murzilli

It seems like a bold idea to build a luxury resort on a stretch of sand beach crossed by a lagoon, swamp and willows that is far, far away from any sort of tourist settlement. The Italian fashion designer, Marcello Murzilli, realized it. As is often the case, the word "hotel" is inappropriate here. "Hotelito" seems much warmer and friendlier. Nevertheless, nothing is left to chance except the natural surroundings. Straight paths, well-selected antiques from all over Mexico, the bar filled with colorful lanterns and the restaurant with deck on the lagoon, the spa complex, the observation tower, beach pavilion and the "palafito" bungalows themselves: the handwriting of the fashion designer is like a label throughout the entire complex. With 29 accommodations that are scattered across two of the total of 40 hectare compound, privacy is ensured at least in a certain sense. Because the walls made of woven bast-fibers are thin, the shutters are attached to a rope over the window openings and the doors to the terrace, thank goodness, are air permeable. There is an unrestricted view from the open air showers and baths—and vice versa. Electric lights have been banned in favor of candelabras and candles. Only the ceiling fan above the mosquito net is powered by electricity. Hotelito is not only an ideal retreat for romantics, but also a colorful, natural experience and a memory of its primitive beauty.

An einer mit Lagunen, Sumpf und Weiden durchzogenen Sandstrand-küste weit weg von jedweder touristischen Ansiedlung ein Luxusresort zu errichten, scheint eine kühne Idee zu sein. Der italienische Modedesigner Marcello Murzilli hat sie verwirklicht. Wie so oft passt auch hier das Wort Hotel nicht wirklich. Hotelito klingt da schon viel wärmer und menschli-cher. Trotzdem ist außer der Naturkulisse nichts dem Zufall überlassen. Akkurate Pfade, gut ausgewählte Antiquitäten aus ganz Mexiko, die farbenprächtige, mit Windlichtern gefüllte Bar und das Restaurant mit Deck an der Lagune, die Spa-Anlage, der Beobachtungsturm, Strand-pavillon und die Wohnhütten selbst: Die Handschrift des Modeschöpfers zieht sich wie ein roter Faden durch die ganze Anlage. Mit nur 29 Wohn-einheiten, die zudem noch auf rund zwei des insgesamt 40 Hektar großen Geländes verstreut sind, ist Privatheit zumindest in gewissem Sinne garantiert. Denn die Wände aus geflochtenem Bast sind dünn, die an einer Schnur hängenden Klappen der Fensterluken leicht, die Türen zur Terrasse zum Glück luftdurchlässig. Bad und Dusche bieten einen unver-bauten Blick ins Freie – und umgekehrt. Elektrisches Licht ist zugunsten von Kandelabern und Kerzen verbannt. Einzig der Ventilator über dem Moskitonetz wird von Strom betrieben. Hotelito ist also nicht nur das ideale Rückzugsgebiet für Romantiker, sondern auch anschauliches Natur-erlebnis und Erinnerung an die Schönheit des Einfachen.

01 | It does without electricity: The Hotelito Desconocido.

Verzichtet auf Elektrizität: das Hotelito Desconocido.

02 | 03

02 | 03 In contrast to the initial impression, the Hotelito Desconocido is not a hangout for hippies but a special kind of hotel for ecologically-minded travelers. A little flower power still drifts through the rooms.

Im Gegensatz zum ersten Eindruck ist das Hotelito Desconocido keine Hippie-Absteige, sondern ein Hotel der besonderen Art für umweltbewusste Reisende. Ein bisschen Flower Power weht dennoch durch die Räume.

04 | 05

06

04 | To be on the safe side, be sure to bring along a flashlight–there is only candlelight in the Hotelito after sundown.

Sicherheitshalber eine Taschenlampe einpacken - im Hotelito brennt nach Einbruch der Dunkelheit nur Kerzenlicht.

05 | Bedroom.

Schlafzimmer.

06 | The parks surrounding the hotel invite guests to take a stroll.

Die Grünanlagen um das Hotel laden zu Spaziergängen ein.

el tamarindo | jalisco . mexico

DESIGN: Architect Luis Bosoms, CEO of Grupo Plan

The heart of El Tamarindo is the 18-hole golf course designed by Robert Trent Jones and David Flemming—without exaggerating, it is one of the most fascinating in the world. It sends the balls and the players through tropical forests, across hilly parks, past rugged cliffs, fine sandy bays, blooming bushes and cacti. The resort has only 28 villas. If you are looking for an intimate setting, you will find the most isolation in the Palm Tree Villas that have two bedrooms or in the Garden or Forest Villas. If you are longing to see another guest walking down the beach once in a while, you will enjoy the Beachfront Villa. All of the villas are built in the so-called "palapa"-style: the pointed roofs of the huts are covered with palm leaves. The restaurant has a first class location, view, architecture and menu. There are tables on several levels in various heights and on wooden terraces or stone floors—always with a panorama view of the Playa el Tamarindo Bay. And finally, the spa treatments are unique including a "temascal". This is an experience to cleanse skin deep into the pores. The centuries-old ritual is a mixture of a pleasant mud bath combined with saltwater cleansing as well as a spiritual opening with extreme heat, darkness and beating of the drums.

Das Herzstück des El Tamarindo ist der von Robert Trent Jones, Jr. und David Flemming gestaltete 18-Loch-Platz – ohne Übertreibung einer der faszinierendsten der Welt. Er schickt die Bälle mit ihren Spielern durch tropische Wälder, über hügelige Parkanlagen, vorbei an schroffen Klippen, feinsandigen Buchten, blühenden Büschen und Kakteen. Gerade einmal 28 Villen zählt das Resort. Wer Intimität sucht, findet die größte Abgeschiedenheit in den Palm Tree-Villen, die es auch mit zwei Schlafzimmern gibt, beziehungsweise in den Garden- oder Forest Villen. Wer sich danach sehnt, ab und zu auch einen anderen Gast am Strand entlangspazieren zu sehen, sollte jedoch eine Beachfront-Villa mieten. Alle Villen sind im so genannten Palapastil gebaut: Die Spitzdächer der Hütten sind mit Palmenwedeln bedeckt. Erstklassig in Lage, Aussicht, Architektur und Menü ist das Restaurant. Tische gibt es auf mehreren Ebenen in verschiedenen Höhen und auf Holzterrassen oder Steinböden – stets mit Panoramablick auf die Bucht des Playa el Tamarindo. Und schließlich: Einmalig ist das Spa-Angebot mit angeschlossenem Temascal. Letzteres ist ein Erlebnis mit gesicherter körperlicher Reinigung – porentief. Das jahrhundertealte Ritual ist ein Grenzgang aus wohltuenden Schlammeinseifungen und Salzwassersäuberungen sowie der geistigen Öffnung in Bruthitze, Dunkelheit und mit Trommelgesängen.

01 | The ideal recreational area for non-golfers too: El Tamarindo.

Auch für Nicht-Golfer ein idealer Erholungsort: Das El Tamarindo.

02 | 03

02 | 03 The temascal cleansing ritual practiced in the Tamarindo Spa is not for those who are faint of heart. Your participation is not required and the spa is a true experience in any case.

Das im Spa des Tamarindo ausgeübte Temascal Reinigungsritual ist nichts für zart besaitete Gemüter. Die Teilnahme ist jedoch nicht zwingend, und so wird das Spa unter allen Umständen zu einem Erlebnis.

04 | The selection of the suite should cater to the guests' need for privacy. The Palm Tree Villa offers the most isolation.

Die Wahl der Suite sollte entsprechend dem Bedürfnis des Gastes nach Gesellschaft getroffen werden. Größte Abgeschiedenheit bieten die Palm Tree-Villen.

01 | It is even possible to swim unobserved–the beach is very nearby.

Auch unbeobachtetes Schwimmen ist möglich – der Strand ist ganz in der Nähe.

el careyes | jalisco . mexico
DESIGN: Diego Villasenor, Grupo Plan

The buildings of the El Careyes placed in the shape of a horseshoe surround the garden with a swimming pool directly adjacent to the beach—a pool with twists and turns as if the designers had simply let a huge drop of water fall down out of a fire-fighting plane. The Grupo Plan, the new owners since 1998, and the management group, Luxury Collection by Starwood have in the meanwhile provided for bold colors and rough edges, that were up to now either painted with light pastels or whitewashed, and alcoves or some wall segments have been complementarily emphasized. The tables of the restaurant are scattered around the covered bar to terraces of various heights. Whether you are sitting at breakfast, lunch or by moon light, you always have a view of the sea and the two headlands of the bay as well as the tiny islands and the rocks rising up out of the water. Even fries with ketchup would be a gourmet dish in this setting. In addition to the usual massage therapies, the spa area emphasizes preventative medicine, or in other words: conscious and healthy living. The beginning is holistic, from the proper diet, to exercise and relaxation with yoga, massages and aroma therapy.

Die hufeisenförmig angeordneten Gebäude des El Careyes umschließen den direkt an den Strand angrenzenden Garten mit Poolanlage – ein Schwimmbecken mit Kurven und Windungen, als ob die Planer aus einem Löschflugzeug einen großen Tropfen nach unten hätten plumpsen lassen. Die seit 1998 neuen Besitzer Grupo Plan und die betreibende Managementgesellschaft Luxury Collection von Starwood haben die bis dato mit zarten Pastelltönen gewischten und weiß gestrichenen Wände in der Zwischenzeit mit kräftigeren Farben und Kanten versehen, Aussparungen oder einige Mauerabschnitte komplementär betont. Die Tische des Restaurants verteilen sich um die überdachte Bar bis hin zu den verschieden hohen Terrassen. Das Meer und die beiden Landzungen der Bucht sowie die dazwischen liegenden Miniinseln und Wasserfelsen hat man dabei stets im Blick, ob zum Frühstück, zur Mittagszeit oder bei Mondschein. In dieser Umgebung werden selbst Pommes mit Ketchup zum Gourmetgericht. Neben den üblichen Massagevariationen liegt im Spabereich ein Schwerpunkt auf präventiver Medizin oder einfacher ausgedrückt: bewusstes und gesundes Leben. Der Ansatz ist ganzheitlich, von der richtigen Ernährung, über Bewegung und Entspannungsübungen mit Yoga, Massagen und Aromatherapie.

02

02 | View from one of the five ocean front junior suites.

Blick aus einer der fünf Ozean-Front-Junior Suiten.

03 | Dining is the shade of the veranda is very pleasant.

Im Schatten der Veranda lässt es sich angenehm speisen.

04 | A small passage with boutiques is located between the hotel and the apartment buildings.

Zwischen Hotel und Apartmentgebäude befindet sich eine kleine Passage mit Boutiquen.

05 | The junior suites have an ocean view. The white blinds ensure a comfortable temperature as in all of the other rooms.

Die Junior-Suiten zeigen direkt aufs Meer. Wie in allen anderen Räumen sorgen auch hier weiße Lamellenläden für eine angenehme Raumtemperatur.

habita | mexico city . mexico

DESIGN: Enrique Norten, Bernardo Gómez-Pimienta, TEN Arquitectos

Since it was founded in the 14th century, Mexico City has grown immensely and with approximately 20 million inhabitants it is now one of the largest cities in the world. Of course, a cumulation of so many people in a relatively small area is always a social focus, at the same time a fertile ground for pulsating life and creativity. Given the size and the potential, it is almost incredible that, with the habita, a design-oriented boutique hotel first appeared on the scene in the year 2000. In contrast to the almost immeasurable sensory stimuli of the city, it makes use of its zen-like simplicity and becomes like a work of art itself. The rooms are designed without colors for the most part: curtain, walls and linens are completely white, tabletops made of glass and simply detailed chairs made of wood and metal have an almost dematerializing effect. The rooms have their own unique atmosphere. After sun bathing, sauna, jogging on the tread-mill or a massage, you can have a drink at the pool bar. Or if you go one level higher, to the hotspot deck of the city: dark wooden floors, with them exposed concrete, white upholstery and crystal-blue glass create a coolness here that is rare in this purity.

Mexiko City ist seit ihrer Gründung im 14. Jahrhundert beträchtlich gewachsen und mit rund zwanzig Millionen Einwohnern mittlerweile eine der größten Städte der Welt. Natürlich ist eine Kumulation von so vielen Menschen auf relativ engem Raum immer auch sozialer Brennpunkt, genauso aber ein fruchtbarer Nährboden für pulsierendes Leben und Kreativitat. Gemessen an der Größe und dem Potenzial ist es fast schon erstaunlich, dass mit dem Habita erst 2000 ein designbetontes Boutique-hotel die Szene bereichert. Gegen die schier überwältigende Reizfülle der Stadt setzt es seine beinahe zenartige Einfachheit und wird damit selbst fast zu einem Kunstwerk. Die Räume sind überwiegend ohne Farben gestaltet: Vorhänge, Wände und Bettwäsche sind vollkommen weiß, Tischplatten aus Glas und sparsam detaillierte Stühle aus Holz und Metall wirken nahezu entmaterialisiert. Die Zimmer besitzen eine eigentümliche Atmosphäre, vor allem der Blick gegen die in weiten Teilen undurchsich-tige Glashaut des Gebäudes erzeugt eine von der Realität losgelöste, fast raumschiffartige Atmosphäre. Nach Sonnenbad, Sauna, Laufbandjogging oder Massage kann man an der Poolbar einen Drink nehmen. Oder aber man begibt sich gleich eine Etage höher, auf das Hotspot-Deck der Stadt: Dunkler Holzfußboden, dazu Sichtbeton, weiße Polster und eisblaues Glas schaffen hier eine angenehm kühle und klare Stimmung, die in dieser Reinheit selten ist.

01 | The impressive, 13 feet long fireplace seems somewhat
uncomfortable, rather matter-of-fact and consistent.

Der beeindruckende, vier Meter lange Kamin wirkt hier weniger
gemütlich, sondern sachlich und konsequent.

02 | Breakfast can be enjoyed on the sun deck by the pool. From the fifth floor, you have a lovely view of the surrounding quarter.

Auf dem Sonnendeck gleich bei dem Pool kann morgens bereits das Frühstück eingenommen werden. Im fünften Stock hat man einen schönen Blick über das angrenzende Viertel.

03 | The hotel is completely enclosed in a skin of glass that filters out all the disturbing impulses and always allows the rooms to appear in their best light.

Das Hotel ist vollständig von einer Glashaut umschlossen, die alle störenden Reize herausfiltert und die Räume stets im besten Licht erscheinen lässt.

04 | The rooftop landscape that the TEN Arquitectos created for the Habita is separated on two levels and is one of the architectural main attractions of the hotel.

Die auf zwei Ebenen verteilte Dachlandschaft, die die TEN Arquitectos für das Habita kreiert haben, ist eine der baulichen Hauptattraktionen des Hotels.

02

03

sheraton centro histórico | mexico city . mexico

DESIGN: Pascal Arquitectos

This hotel overlooking Alameda Park has 457 guest rooms, most of which offer great views of the city's downtown district including the 394-feet skyscraper, Torre Latinoamericana, and picturesque Palacio de Bellas Artes. This makes it the ideal base for guests looking to explore Mexico City's historic center. Right next door is the Museo de Arte Popular recently opened in 2006 newly, designed by Teodoro González de León. Just a few steps away, visitors find the Museo Mural Diego Rivera with its huge wall painting "Dream of a Sunday afternoon in the Alameda-Park". Not more than 10 minutes walking distance there is the heart of the national Mexican identity, the world famous Zócalo square, which is surrounded by the Presidential Palace, the historical City Hall, as well as the world's largest baroque church Catedral Metropolitana. From the grand atrium of the 27-story hotel, guests find two different levels of restaurants, bars and shops, as well as the conference center. Although it was built as a conference hotel with accommodations for up to 2,000 people, its contemporary architecture, color scheme and design concept evoke a luxurious relaxed club atmosphere. Those who want to completely escape from city life will find a personal oasis in the sixth floor. Here is the brand new 32.000-square feet wellness center, with an indoor and an approximate 80-feet outdoor pool, rooftop sun deck, terrace restaurant, gym and spa presented all here as an architectural piece of art in a minimalist space.

Wer das historische Zentrum der Stadt erkunden möchte, dem gewähren bereits die meisten der 457 Zimmer Aussicht auf den Alameda Park und „Downtown" mit seinem 182 Meter hohen Torre Latinoamericana oder dem pittoresken „Palacio de Bellas Artes" (Palast der Schönen Künste). Unmittelbar angrenzend an das Hotel ist das von Teodoro González de León geplante und 2006 neu eröffnete Museo de Arte Popular, nur ein paar Schritte entfernt das Museo Mural Diego Riviera mit dem riesigen Wandbild „Traum eines Sonntagnachmittags im Alameda-Park". Zu Fuß sind es nur 10 Minuten zum weltberühmten Zócalo Platz, der umsäumt ist vom Präsidentenpalast, dem historischen Rathaus sowie der weltgrößten Barockkirche Catedral Metropolitana. Mittelpunkt des 27-geschossigen Hotelhochhauses ist die Atrium-Lobby, in der auf zwei Etagen Restaurants, Cafeteria, Shops und Bars sowie die Veranstaltungsräume untergebracht sind. Obwohl als Kongresszentrum für bis zu 2000 Personen angelegt, erzeugt die zeitgenössische Architektur mit ihrem Farb- und Materialkonzept eine entspannte Clubatmosphäre. Wer sich jedoch ganz aus dem städtischen Umtrieb verabschieden möchte, findet seine Oase in dem 2006 eröffneten, 3000 Quadratmeter großen Wellnesszentrum im sechsten Obergeschoss. Hallenschwimmbad und über 25 m langes Außenbecken, Dachgarten mit Sonnenterrasse und Restaurant, Fitnessräume sowie ein hypermodernes Spa präsentieren sich als minimalistisch-architektonisches Gesamtkunstwerk.

01 | On the left is the reception and hotel bar, on the right a tasty traditional Mexican restaurant, wine tasting bistro and a coffee shop. In the gallery are the entrances to the conference rooms.

Links befinden sich die Rezeption und Hotelbar, rechts unten ein mexikanisches Spezialitätenrestaurant, eine Vinothek sowie ein Coffeshop, die Galerie der oberen Etage führt zu den Veranstaltungsräumen.

02 | The sixth floor combines all the essentials elements for wellness, health and sports, like the steam bath with view to a tropical garden.

Dampfbad mit Blick in einen kleinen Tropengarten. Alles in der sechsten Hoteletage.

03 | Here you will find minimalist architecture in the spa area and a serene hallway guiding you to the treatment rooms.

Minimalistische Architektur im Spa. Hier einer der Flure, die zu den Behandlungsräumen führen.

04 | **05** Mexico City as far as the eye can see. The views from the rooms on the upper levels of this 27-story skyscraper give you an idea of just how vast this bustling metropolis really is.

Mexico City so weit das Auge reicht. Beim Blick aus den Zimmern der höheren Etagen des 27-stöckigen Hochhauses bekommt man ein Gefühl für die Größe der Millionenmetropole.

03 04
05

four seasons resort costa rica | peninsula papagayo . costa rica

DESIGN: Richard Brayton from Brayton + Hughes, San Francisco; Ronald Zurcher of Zurcher Arquitectos

Each of the 153 suites in this paradise for eco-tourists is nestled into the hilly landscape and blends into the environment. Large, sliding doors give an unrestricted view of the natural beauty of the area: sea, sunshine beaches and forests. The colors of this view are also found in the rooms: earthy tones and the colors of the indigenous trees emphasize the design of the rooms. The two-story spa offers relaxation on over 16.100 square feet after excursions to the natural attractions of the rain forest, volcanoes and national parks. Treatments, that are unique for Costa Rica, for example mineral-rich mud packs from the rain forest of the nearby Osa Peninsula, are offered in the gently lit rooms. In addition to the spa, the Four Seasons Costa Rica also offers numerous sporting activities. Guests can either train in the hotel fitness center or hit a few balls: on the golf course or tennis court according to your tastes. Even if you bring the kids along, you do not have to deny yourself the athletic challenges. The Four Seasons Costa Rica, as in many other Four Seasons hotels, offers a variety of programs even for the youngest guests.

Jede der 153 Suiten in diesem Paradies für Ökotouristen ist in die Hügellandschaft eingebettet und verschmilzt mit der Umgebung. Große Schiebetüren geben den Blick auf die Naturschönheiten der Gegend frei: Meer, sonnenbeschienene Strände und Wälder. Die Farben dieses Ausblicks finden sich auch in den Zimmern wieder: Erdtöne und die Farben der heimischen Bäume bestimmen das Design der Räume. Der zweistöckige Spabereich bietet auf 1500 Quadratmetern Entspannung nach Exkursionen zu den Naturattraktionen des Regenwaldes, der Vulkane und Nationalparks. In sanft beleuchteten Räumen werden Behandlungen angeboten, die einzigartig sind für Costa Rica, etwa mineralreiche Schlammpackungen aus dem Regenwald der nahen Osa-Halbinsel. Neben dem Spa bietet das Four Seasons Costa Rica auch zahlreiche sportliche Aktivitäten an. Die Gäste können entweder im Fitness-Studio des Hotels trainieren, oder ein paar Bälle schlagen: je nach Geschmack auf dem Golfplatz oder auf dem Tenniscourt. Auch wenn man Kinder mitbringt, müssen die sportlichen Herausforderungen nicht abgelehnt werden, denn wie in vielen anderen Four Seasons Häusern wird ein reichhaltiges Programm selbst für die kleinsten Gäste angeboten.

01 | The view from the balcony of one of the Four Seasons Costa Rica's 153 suites.

Blick vom Balkon einer der 153 Suiten des Four Seasons Costa Rica.

02 | Guests have plenty of room in the spa: The 16.100 square feet of spa area offer a meditative atmosphere and relaxation.

Im Spa hat man reichlich Auslauf: Die 1500 Quadratmeter bieten meditative Stimmung und Erholung.

03 | The rooms' furnishings are coordinated to the colors of the flora and fauna surrounding the Four Seasons Costa Rica..

Die Einrichtung der Zimmer orientiert sich an den Farben der Flora und Fauna um das Four Seasons Costa Rica.

04 | Dining on one of the hotel terraces seems like a picnic in the rain forest. Those who wish to take a walk on the wild side can participate in tours to the attractions of the nearby nature parks.

Wie ein Picknick im Regenwald erscheint ein Essen auf einer der Hotelterrassen. Wer sich in wilde Natur wagen möchte, kann an Touren zu den Attraktionen der nahegelegenen Naturparks teilnehmen.

pousada picinguaba | picinguaba . brazil

DESIGN: Emmanuel Rengade, Christina Andrade, Kurt Reiner

Only rarely does a tropical rain forest border so closely on the coast of the ocean as in the "Mata Atlantica" National Park in Brazil. Its indescribable flora and fauna form the coastal layout between Rio and São Paulo. A place of tranquility and absolute proximity to the original Brazil. The fine, exclusive Pousada Picinguaba is situated in the middle of these tropical gardens and offers an ideal location to relax with ten spacious guest rooms including the honeymoon suite. Guests literally bath in natural riches with the sea to the left and the fertile fauna to the right. Even the crystal-clear water of the swimming pool is served by a source in the tropical forest. The Pousada, with its bright colors and natural style is a homage to the artist and the traditions of the land. A place that honors the land in its many facets. The bar and restaurant conjure up a large, fresh selection of local specialties and delicacies daily. There is indeed an irresistible attraction of taking a time out in the middle of this lush landscape where a seamless transition exists between the mountains and the sea. For some, the rainforest adventure lies just beyond the door. Marine enthusiasts can have themselves taken with the hotel boat to the most beautiful beaches on the coast or simply enjoy the Brazilian way of life from onboard the boat.

Nur selten grenzt ein tropischer Regenwald so nah an die Ufer des Ozeans wie der Nationalpark „Mata Atlantica" in Brasilien. Seine unbeschreibliche Flora und Fauna prägen das Küstenbild zwischen Rio und São Paulo. Ein Ort der Ruhe und absoluten Nähe zum ursprünglichen Brasilien. Die feine, exklusive Pousada Picinguaba ist inmitten dieses tropischen Gartens situiert und bietet mit zehn großzügigen Gästezimmern inklusive Hochzeitssuite einen idealen Ort der Erholung. Das Meer zur Linken, die fruchtbare Fauna zur Rechten baden die Gäste sprichwörtlich in natürlichem Reichtum. Selbst das klare Wasser des Swimming-Pools speist sich aus einer Quelle des tropischen Waldes. Die Pousada ist in ihrem farbenfrohen und natürlichen Stil eine wunderbare Hommage an die Künstler und die Traditionen des Landes. Ein Ort, der das Land in all seinen Facetten ehrt. So zaubern Bar und Restaurant eine große Palette an lokalen Spezialitäten und Köstlichkeiten täglich frisch auf den Tisch. Der Reiz inmitten dieser üppigen Landschaft eine Auszeit zu nehmen, wo der Übergang zwischen den Bergen und dem Meer fließend ist, ist verlockend. Für den einen liegt das Abenteuer Regenwald direkt vor der Tür. Meer-Enthusiasten lassen sich mit dem hauseigenen Boot zu den schönsten Stränden der Küste fahren oder genießen von der Bootsseite aus den brasilianischen Way of Life.

01 | The natural material used for the furnishings give the hotel a pristine flair.

Die bei der Einrichtung verwendeten Naturmaterialien verleihen dem Hotel ursprüngliches Flair.

02 | Even long forgotten games like Halma are fun again in the cozy atmosphere of the rooms.

In der gemütlichen Atmosphäre der Zimmer machen sogar längst vergessene Spielklassiker wie Halma auf einmal wieder Spaß.

03 | The pool of the Pousada Picinguaba.

Der Pool des Pousada Picinguaba.

04 | Filled with gentle light, in the rooms of this retreat on the edge of the rain forest , life is light and easy-going like in a Gilberto/Getz song.

Leicht und unbeschwert wie ein Gilberto/Getz Song ist das Leben in den von sanftem Licht erhellten Räumen dieses Rückzugsortes an der Grenze zum Regenwald.

emiliano | são paulo . brazil

DESIGN: Arthur Casas

This narrow, architectonically–impressive building sticks up like a finger out of the best quarter in São Paulo, where designers shops and banks from all over the world present themselves. In the Emiliano, you are well-prepared for the clientele from this kind of district. The Emiliano welcomes guests with a 15-minute massage in order to prepare them for the five star service awaiting them during their entire stay. Each guest should feel right at home here—only better. Drinks tailored to the guest's personal tastes wait in the mini bar and newspapers from all over the world can be brought to the rooms upon request. In the upper part of the building, the hotel waits with its 38 large rooms and 19 suites that are even larger; the bathrooms are all furnished with Carrara marble. Those who prefer to let themselves be pampered by skilled therapists using precious oils will certainly enjoy the Emiliano. The hotel has its own spa designed according to the principles of Feng Shui with a view of the city. The classic-modern restaurant with its exquisite Italian cuisine as well as the bar with its extraordinary design are further highlights of the hotel. When relaxing in the spa, the view from the top floor is also unique.

Das schmale, architektonisch eindrucksvolle Gebäude ragt wie ein Finger aus dem besten Viertel São Paulos auf, wo sich Designläden und Banken aus aller Welt präsentieren. Auf das Publikum dieses Viertels ist man im Emiliano bestens vorbereitet. Um die Gäste wiederum auf den Fünf-Sterne-Service vorzubereiten, der sie während ihres ganzen Aufenthalts umgeben wird, empfängt das Emiliano seine Besucher mit einer fünfzehn-minütigen Willkommensmassage. Ganz wie zu Hause soll sich hier jeder Gast fühlen – nur besser. In der Minibar warten auf den persönlichen Geschmack abgestimmte Getränke, und auf Wunsch werden Zeitungen aus aller Welt in den Zimmern bereitgelegt. Im oberen Teil des Gebäudes wartet das Hotel mit 38 großen Zimmern und 19 noch größeren Suiten auf; die Badezimmer sind allesamt mit Carraramarmor ausgestattet. Diejenigen, die es bevorzugen, sich nicht nur selber zu pflegen sondern, sich von fremden Händen beispielsweise mit kostbaren Ölen behandeln zu lassen, werden am Emiliano ihr Freude haben: Das Hotel verfügt über ein nach Feng Shui-Kriterien eingerichtetes Spa mit Blick über die ganze Stadt. Glanzstücke der Adresse sind das klassisch-moderne Restaurant mit feiner italienischer Küche sowie die Bar mit ungewöhnlichem Design. Als einzigartig erweist sich zudem der Ausblick beim Relaxen in dem Spa in der obersten Etage.

01 | The spa offers not only relaxation but also insights into the most modern architecture.

Das Spa bietet nicht nur Entspannung, sondern auch Einblicke in modernste Architektur.

02 | After an exciting day in the streets of São Paulo, a calm atmosphere waits in the lobby.

Nach einem aufregenden Tag in São Paulo wartet eine ruhige Atmosphäre in der Lobby.

03 | After the welcome massage, the guests will find international newspapers and a cozy atmosphere in the guest rooms.

Nach einer Willkommensmassage erwarten die Hotelzimmer die Gäste mit internationalen Zeitschriften und heimeliger Atmosphäre.

04 | Muted creme and earth tones make the room bright but not loud.

Gedeckte Creme- und Erdtöne lassen die Zimmer hell, aber nicht grell wirken.

05 | Precious materials such as Carrara marble were used for the bathrooms.

Für die Bäder wurden edelste Materialien wie Carraramarmor verwendet.

06 | Through its use of greenery in the inner court yard, the Emiliano almost becomes a small city with a park in the middle. When you are finished admiring this, don't forget to check out some of São Paulo as well.

Durch den begrünten Innenhof wird das Emiliano beinahe zu einer Art kleinen Stadt mit einem Park in der Mitte. Wer diesen genug bewundert hat, sollte nicht versäumen, auch noch etwas in São Paulo zu erleben.

01 | Renowned beyond the borders of Uruguay: The Colony Park Plaza Spa.

Weit über die Grenzen Uruguays bekannt: das Spa des Colony Park Plaza.

kempinski hotel colony park plaza | colonia del sacramento . uruguay
DESIGN: Jorge Felly

The Kempinski Hotel Colony Park Plaza in Uruguay presents itself architectonically in an elegant and modern look to its guests. Located in the middle of the paradise-like landscape of the Rio de la Plata, close to the historical center of Ciudad de Colonia, it waits with its five star service that is an international standard. The 86 guest rooms, among them 53 superior and 25 deluxe accommodations, as well as one suite deluxe have a comfortable and individual appearance. All the rooms lead out to a generous, adjoining terrace with unique panorama view of the foothills of the Andes and the lush river landscape of the mighty Rio de la Plata. The name Kempinski stands for relaxation on the highest level. The Spa and Resort Hotel takes up an adequate amount of space as well. An underground passageway leads from the main building to an enormous wellness park that is spread out over an area of around 2.500 square meters. It is one of the finest spas in South America with its exclusive furnishings and is renowned outside of Uruguay as a center of health, beauty and wellness. An ideal place for guests who have earned a break and are seeking rejuvenation of the body and mind. The fare by Colony by Kempinski Restaurant makes it a culinary experience.

Architektonisch präsentiert sich das Kempinski Hotel Colony Park Plaza in Uruguay seinen Gästen in einem eleganten und modernen Gewand. Gelegen inmitten der traumhaften Landschaft des Rio de la Plata, unweit des historischen Zentrums von Ciudad de Colonia wartet es mit einem Fünf-Sterne-Service auf, der den internationalen Maßstäben entspricht. Die 86 Gästezimmern darunter 53 Superior- und 25 Deluxe-Unterkünfte sowie eine Suite Deluxe, präsentieren sich dem Gast in einem individuellen und komfortablen Erscheinungsbild. Alle Zimmer führen auf eine großzügig angelegte Terrasse mit einem einzigartigen Blick über die weiten Gebirgszüge der Anden und die üppige Flusslandschaft des mächtigen Rio de la Plata. Kempinski steht für Erholung auf höchstem Niveau. Entsprechend viel Raum nimmt das Spa & Resort Hotels ein. Eine unterirdische Passage führt vom Haupthaus in einen riesigen Wellness-Park, der sich auf einer Fläche von rund 2500 Quadratmetern erstreckt. Mit seiner exklusiven Ausstattung gehört er zu den besten Spa-Welten Südamerikas und ist als Zentrum für Gesundheit, Schönheit und Wohlbefinden über die Grenzen Uruguays hinaus bekannt. Ein idealer Platz für Gäste, die sich eine Auszeit gönnen und Erholung für Körper und Geist suchen. Die leichte Küche des Colony by Kempinski Restaurant macht dies zu einem kulinarisch exquisiten Erlebnis.

02 | 03 High ceilings, elegant furnishings, polished floors–the Colony
Park Plaza is as prestigious as any other renowned international
hotel.

Hohe Räume, elegante Einrichtung, polierte Böden – das Colony
Park Plaza macht auf dem internationalen Hotel-Parkett keine
schlechte Figur.

04 | There was no time for fun and games when designing the hotel.
A sense of earnest is evoked through the use of dark woods.

Beim Hoteldesign nahm man sich keine Zeit für Spielereien.
Durch die Verwendung von dunklen Hölzern kommt eine seriöse
Stimmung auf.

04

05 | The interior calls to mind an elegant mansion from 1900, whose technical features have kept in step with the times.

Das Interieur erinnert vielfach an ein vornehmes Herrenhaus um 1900, dessen technische Ausstattung mit der Zeit gegangen ist.

faena hotel + universe | buenos aires . argentina
DESIGN: Philippe Starck, Faena Group

When you enter the hotel, you could almost imagine that you have found your way into a design exhibit: the entrance itself already seems like a temple dedicated to good taste. Alan Faena, founder of the fashion label, Via Vai, created a lifestyle universe unique for Buenos Aires from a old grain storage silo. There is also a hint of belle-epoche mixed into the design by Philippe Starck, apparent in the white-gold pomp of the bistro and the furniture. All of this does not mean that the result is a sterile museum atmosphere that always leaves one fearing that something could get dirty or destroyed just by one's presence alone. And even if that were the case: the service staff would eliminate any evidence so quickly that one would not even notice the faux pas himself. The features of this hotel such as stage, spa, boutique and pool bar are taken for granted by the managers and the standards are equally as high with which the guest is surrounded in these accommodations. The pool area looks a little as if someone let Snow White do the decorating: the snow-white hand towels meet the blood-red lounge chairs that are grouped around the swimming pool. So every woman can feel like an undiscovered princess and every man like a king especially when he is served a delectable Argentinean steak while sitting in his white leather throne in the restaurant.

Fast könnte man beim Betreten des Hotels glauben, man sei in eine Design-Ausstellung geraten: Bereits das Entrée wirkt wie eine Kathedrale, die dem guten Geschmack huldigt. Alan Faena, Gründer des Modelabels Via Vai, erschuf aus einem alten Getreidespeicher ein für Buenos Aires bisher einmaliges Lifestyle-Universum. In das Design von Philippe Starck mischt sich ein Hauch von Belle Epoque, sichtbar am weiß-goldenen Pomp des Bistros und dem Mobiliar. All das bedeutet aber nicht, dass eine sterile Museumsatmosphäre entsteht, die ständig fürchten lässt, man könnte allein mit seiner Anwesenheit etwas schmutzig machen oder zerstören. Und selbst wenn: Das Servicepersonal hätte so schnell alle Spuren beseitigt, dass man seinen Fauxpas selbst nicht bemerken würde. Die Features des Hotels wie Bühne, Spa, Boutique und Poolbar werden von den Betreibern selber als Selbstverständlichkeiten angesehen, und entsprechend hoch sind auch die Standards, mit denen der Gast sich in diesen Räumlichkeiten umgibt. Der Poolbereich sieht ein wenig so aus, als hätte man Schneewittchen die Farbwahl treffen lassen: Das Schneeweiß der Handtücher trifft auf das Blutrot der Sonnenliegen, die um den Pool gruppiert sind. So darf sich jede Frau wie eine unentdeckte Prinzessin fühlen, und jeder Mann wie ein König, spätestens dann, wenn ihm auf einem der weißen Lederthrone des Restaurants ein köstliches argentinisches Steak serviert wird.

01 | The "blue as the earth" color defines the spa in the Faena Universe.

Planetenblau bestimmt das Spa im Faena Universe.

02 03

04

02 | Don't be afraid of kitsch! Fans of an overboard baroque design are right at home in the Faena Universe Restaurant.

Keine Angst vor Kitsch! Freunde eines barock-überbordenden Designs sind im Restaurant Faena Universe bestens aufgehoben.

03 | After a shopping tour in the hotel's boutiques, stop by the pool for a quick refresher.

Ein paar Minuten im Pool erfrischen nach einer Einkaufstour in der hauseigenen Boutique.

04 | In contrast to the restaurant, the suites of the hotel are free of unnecessary detail. Snow white and rose red are the only colors used in for the furnishings.

Im Gegensatz zum Restaurant sind die Suiten des Hotels frei von verspielten Details. Schneeweißchen und Rosenrot sind aber auch hier die Farbpatinnen der Einrichtung.

palacio duhau park hyatt buenos aires | buenos aires . argentinien

DESIGN: Roberto Caparra, Cora Entelman, Guillermo Petrocchi, Andrea Contegrand, Enrique Dieguez, Sra Marta Priu

Buenos Aires is not only the birthplace of the Tango. The city with its large population is a metropolis of contradictions; tradition and modern blend together like in no other city. The most exclusive hotel, the Palacio Duhau, does not try to distance itself from this melting pot. Located in the middle of the pulsating city life in the exclusive "Recoleta" district, it reflects an important symbiosis between the historical past of Buenos Aires and the ultramodern design and comfort. It is the district of the rich and beautiful people in Buenos Aires. A district of unbroken youth and vitality, with the wonderful lightness of French flair. Boutiques, galleries and art stores stand together in a row like pearls in the famous Avenida Alvear in which the Palacio is also located. An elaborate garden, whose high standards meet those of this palace, greets the guests upon their arrival. The Duhau offers first class comfort and design in its 165 exclusive guestrooms. The technical equipment, in addition to the basic features, provides business travelers with high speed internet access. Yet who can think of work when the hotel promises relaxation with its spa oasis on over 750 square meters and the unobstructed view of the garden and the lively city is so inviting. A fitness center, heated indoor swimming pool, sauna and separate whirlpool ensure a wellness experience around the clock.

Buenos Aires ist nicht nur die Wiege des Tangos. Die Millionenstadt ist eine Metropole der Widersprüche, in der Tradition und Moderne wie in kaum einer anderen Stadt miteinander verschmelzen. Auch das exklusivste Hotel am Platz, das Palacio Duhau, will sich diesem Schmelztiegel nicht entziehen. Inmitten des pulsierenden Lebens, im angesagten Wohnviertel "Recoleta" gelegen, spiegelt es eine imposante Symbiose zwischen der historischen Vergangenheit Buenos Aires und hochmodernem Design und Komfort wider. Es ist das Viertel der Schönen und Reichen Buenos Aires. Ein Viertel von ungebrochener Jugendlichkeit und Vitalität, mit der wunderbaren Leichtigkeit französischen Flairs. Boutiquen, Galerien und Kunstgewerbeläden reihen sich wie Perlen in der berühmten Straße Avenida Alvear aneinander, in der sich der Palacio befindet. Ein prachtvoller Garten empfängt seine Gäste, deren hohen Ansprüchen dieser Palast voll und ganz entsprechen kann. In 165 exklusiven Gästezimmern bietet das Duhau Komfort und Design der Spitzenklasse. Die technologische Ausstattung hält neben der Grundausstattung einen High Speed Internetzugang für alle Geschäftsreisenden bereit. Doch wer denkt ans Arbeiten, wenn das Hotel mit einer Spa-Oase auf 750 Quadratmetern Erholung verspricht und den offenen Blick gern auf den Garten und das lebendige Stadtleben lenkt. Darüber hinaus sorgen ein Fitness-Center, ein beheizter Indoor-Swimmingpool, eine Sauna und ein separater Whirlpool für ein Wellness-Erlebnis rund um die Uhr.

01 | The suites appear even more spacious with the glass between the bath and bedroom.

Durch die Verglasung zwischen Bad und Schlafzimmer wirken die Suiten noch geräumiger.

02 | 03

02 | When having your first café au lait on the terrace, you start to get the impression of being in a French chateau.

Beim ersten Café au lait auf der Terrasse kommen Assoziationen zu einem französischen Château auf.

03 | In the unlikely event that you should become tired of admiring the hotel's design, you can always spend a quiet evening with a good book by the fireplace.

Sollte man wider Erwarten irgendwann genug davon haben, das Design des Hotels zu bewundern, bietet sich ein ruhiger Leseabend am Kamin an.

04 | The ballroom atmosphere in the Duhau – the splendid rooms almost invite you to put on your dancing shoes.

Ballsaal-Atmosphäre im Duhau – die prunkvollen Säle fordern nahezu heraus, sich hier die Schuhe durchzutanzen.

04

hotel index

Country / Location	Address	Information	Architecture & Design	Page
Wyoming — Jackson Hole 	Amangani 1535 North East Butte Road Jackson Hole, WY 83001 USA www.amangani.com	opened 1998 40 suites, with bathroom and fireplace in the living room. Bar, lounge and restaurant, library, pool and whirlpool, fitness rooms, various outdoor facilities near Yellowstone National Park.	Edward Tuttle	8
California — Dana Point 	St. Regis Resort, Monarch Beach One Monarch Beach Resort Dana Point, CA 92629 USA www.stregismb.com	opened 2001 400 rooms, restaurants, bars, lobby lounge, wine cellar, poolside bar and grill, swimming pool, tennis, sports, spa, fitness center. Located on 172 acres overlooking the Pacific Ocean. John Wayne/Orange County Airport 21 miles, Los Angeles International 65 miles and San Diego International 70 miles.	Hirsch Bedner Associates of Santa Monica, California; Holmes & Narver of Orange, California	12
California — Big Sur 	Post Ranch Inn Highway 1 Big Sur, CA 93920 USA www.postranchinn.com	opened 1992 30 guestrooms and tree houses. Restaurant, library, boutique, hiking trail, infinity pool, fitness center, spa, yoga, shiatsu, reiki. Located on a cliff above Big Sur, 30 minutes south of Monterey and 2 hours south of San José International Airport.	Mickey Muennig Janet Gay Freed	16
California — Desert Hot Springs 	Hope Springs 68075 Club Circle Drive Desert Hot Springs CA 92240 USA www.hopespringsresort.com	opened 1999 10 rooms, some with kitchenette, self-service kitchen, lounge and living room. Pools with hot spring water, massage, menu, library with large variety of CDs and books. 15 minutes north of Palm Springs.	Steve & Misako Samiof Mike Haggerty	20
California — Desert Hot Springs 	Sagewater Spa 12689 Eliseo Road Desert Hot Springs CA 92240 USA www.sagewaterspa.com	opened 2001 7 rooms, some with kitchenette, patio, poolside barbecue and DSL internet access. Pool and spa filled with their own hot mineral spring well water, massage menu, 360 degree mountain views. 15 minutes north of Palm Springs.	Rhoni Epstein Cristina Pestana	24

hotel index

Country / Location		Address	Information	Architecture & Design	Page
California	Palm Springs	The Parker Palm Springs 4200 East Palm Canyon Drive, Palm Springs CA 92264 USA www.theparkerpalmsprings.com	opened 2004 131 rooms and 13 villas. Two restaurants and bar, two indoor and two outdoor pools. Spa, tennis, five meeting rooms. Palm Springs Yacht Club. 10 minutes drive from Palm Springs National Airport.	David Mann Jonathan Adler	28
California	San Diego	W San Diego 421 West B Street San Diego, CA 92101 USA www.starwoodhotels.com	opened 2002 258 rooms. Restaurant, spa and pool, situated in the Columbia district of downtown San Diego, near Little Italy.	Jensen-Fey Architecture & Planning Shopworks in cooperation W Design Group	34
Arizona	Scottsdale	Sanctuary on Camelback Mountain 5700 East McDonald Drive, Scottsdale, AZ 85253, USA www.sanctuaryoncamel-back.com	opened 2001 98 luxurious mountain and spa casitas. 200 guests for banquet seating, spa, restaurant. Located 8 miles north of Phoenix Sky Harbor International Airport and less than five minutes from down-town Scottsdale.	Hiriam Hudson Benedict Catherine M. Hayes of Hayes	38
Florida	Miami Beach	Casa Casuarina 1116 Ocean Drive Miami Beach, FL 33139 USA www.casacasuarina.com	opened 2005 10 suites. Private invitation-only membership club. Four Lounges, polo bar, roof deck, overlooking the. Luxury private beach cabanas. Spa with massage, reflexology, acupressure, gemstone therapy. Located near the Ocean Drive. 20 km from Miami Inter-national Airport, 37 km from Fort Lauderdale International Airport.	Eldin Freeman Versace	44
Florida	Miami Beach	The Setai 2001 Collins Avenue Miami Beach, FL 33139 USA www.setai.com	opened 2005 75 studio suites (58 m²), 50 suites (84 m²), penthouse (929 m²) with rooftop pool. Restaurant, lounge, bar and beach bar. Three beachfront pools. Spa with ocean view. Fitness center with personal trainers, yoga, Tai Chi. Golf, tennis, and deep sea diving nearby. Located on the beach of South Beach.	Jaya Pratomo Ibrahim from Jaya & Associates Jean Michel Gathy from Denniston International	48

hotel index

Country / Location		Address	Information	Architecture & Design	Page
Florida	Miami Beach	The Standard Miami 40 Island Avenue Miami Beach, FL 33139 USA www.andrebalazsproperties.com	opened 2006 105 guest rooms with private verandas and outdoor tubs, restaurant and bayside grill, 7 spa rooms, hamam, steam and scrub room, sauna. Indoor and outdoor baths, sound pool with underwater music, yoga, skin care, gym, located on the waters of Belle Isle. 5 minutes from the beach. 15 minutes from Miami Airport. 45 Minutes from Fort Lauderdale Airport.	Shawn Hausman and André Balazs Properties Alison Spear (project architect)	52
Florida	Miami	Mandarin Oriental, Miami 500 Brickell Key Drive Miami, FL 33131 USA www.mandarinoriental.com	opened 2000, grand opening 2001 327 rooms and 31 suites, restaurant, 3 bars. Private beach with swinging hammocks and spa cabanas. infinity edge swimming pool, fitness center. 20 minutes drive from Miami International Airport and 35 minutes drive from Fort Lauderdale Airport.	Hirsch Bedner & Associates Tony Chi & Associates (restaurant design) RTKL Associates	56
New York	New York	Mandarin Oriental, New York 80 Columbus Circle at 60th Street, NY 10023 USA www.mandarinoriental.com	opened 2003 203 rooms and 48 suites on floors 35 to 54 with floor-to-ceiling views. Restaurant and lobby lounge on the 35th floor. 14.500-square feet spa, gym, swimming pool, fitness center. Located at the Columbus Circle on the top of the Time Warner Center at the Central Park. From JFK International Airport 20 minutes, La Guardia Airport 12 minutes, Newark 27 minutes.	Hirsch Bedner & Associates Brennan Beer Gorman, Architects, L.L.P. Tony Chi & Associates (restaurant design)	60
Bahamas	Emerald Bay	Four Seasons Resort Great Exuma P.O. Box EX29005 Queen's Highway, Emerald Bay Great Exuma, The Bahamas www.fourseasons.com	opened 2003 183 rooms, 43 suites with a view on the Emerald Bay. 2 restaurants, surfing, offshore fishing, golf on the 18 hole golf course, spa. 15 minutes to Exuma International, 2 flight hours from Miami.	Smallwood Reynolds Stewart & Stewart Avery Brooks & Associates	64
Bahamas	Paradise Island	One&Only Ocean Club Paradise Island The Bahamas www.oneandonlyresorts.com	reopened 2000/2004 87 rooms, 14 suites, 2 two-bedroom garden cottages, 2 three-bedroom villas and 1 four-bedroom villa. Restaurant, bar, café, terrace, pool, spa, golf course, tennis, fitness and garden. The resort is located on the eastern end of Paradise Island. A 40 minute drive from Nassau International Airport.	Barry Design Associates Hill Glazier Architects Perdian International	68

hotel index

Country / Location	Address	Information	Architecture & Design	Page
Turks and Caicos Isl. Providenciales	Amanyara Northwest Point Providenciales Turks and Caicos Islands, British West Indies www.amanresorts.com	opened 2006 40 pavilions, restaurant, bar, beach club, swimming pools, library, boutique, screening-room, fitness center, tennis courts. Located along the coast of Northwest Point, adjacent to Malcolm's Beach on Providenciales. Transfer from International Airport on Providenciales is 25 minutes.	Team around Jean Michel Gathy	72
Anguilla Maunday's Bay	Cap Juluca P.O. Box 240 Maunday's Bay Anguilla www.capjuluca.com	opened 1998 58 rooms und junior suites, 7 suites, 6 pool villas. Restaurants various sports, windsurfing, sailing, scuba dive, holistic spa treatments.	Oskar Farmer Bob Perkins Xanadu	76
British West Indies Antigua	Carlisle Bay Old Road St. Mary's, Antigua British West Indies www.carlisle-bay.com	opened 2003 80 suites, two restaurants, three bars. Spa with six treatment rooms, sauna, plunge pools, gym, yoga, personal trainers, water sports, tennis. 30 minutes from Antigua International Airport.	Mary Fox Linton Gordon Campbell Gray	80
French West Indies St. Barthélemy	Le Sereno B.P. 19 Grand-Cul-de-Sac 97133 St. Barthélemy French West Indies www.lesereno.com	opened 2005 37 suites and villas. Restaurant, bar and lounge, beachfront freshwater infinity pool, water sports, spa, fitness center, airport transfer. Located in the heart of the French West Indies, 25 km southeast of St. Maarten, 10 minutes from St. Barthélemy Airport.	Christian Liaigre	86
British West Indies Barbados	The House Paynes Bay St. James Barbados British West Indies www.thehousebarbados.com	opened 2001 31 suites. Restaurant, bar, beachfront location, water sports, swimming pools, fitness center, spa. 30 minutes drive from the airport.	Luciano Colombo	92

hotel index

hotel index

hotel index

Country / Location		Address	Information	Architecture & Design	Page
Brazil	São Paulo	Emiliano Rua Oscar Freire 384 São Paulo S/P Brazil www.emiliano.com.br	opened 2001 57 rooms. Restaurant and lobby bar. Spa, steam room, sauna, gym. Business center. Heli pad. Located right in the center of São Paulo. Located at Oscar Freire Street, in the heart of Jardins. 30 km from the Guarulhos International Airport.	Arthur Casas	140
Uruguay	Colonia del Sacramento	Kempinski Hotel Colony Park Plaza Rambla de las Américas y JM Blanes, Colonia del Sacramento, 70000 Uruguay www.colonyparkplaza.com	opened 2003 86 rooms. Restaurant, indoor pool, outdoor heated pool, tennis court, volley ball court. 5 minutes from the Colonia port to the hotel, or 1.5 hours from Montevideo.	Jorge Felly	146
Argentinia	Buenos Aires	Faena Hotel + Universe Martha Salotti 445 (C1107CMB) Buenos Aires Argentina www.faenahotelanduniverse.com	opened 1995 105 rooms and suites. Restaurant, bistro, spa, pool bar, wine cellar, theater and cabaret with live performances daily, business center. Swimming pool, library lounge. Located in the heart of the El Porteno Art District in Puerto Madero, Buenos Aires. 40 minutes from the airport in the Puerto Madero neighborhood of Buenos Aires.	Philippe Starck Faena Group	152
Argentina	Buenos Aires	Palacio Duhau Park Hyatt Buenos Aires Avenida Alvear 1661 Buenos Aires, C1014AAD Argentina www.buenosaires.park.hyatt.com	opened 2006 165 rooms. 3 restaurants, bar, spa, wine library, cheese room. 36 km from Buenos Aires International Airport. 2 km from Pier of Buenos Aires.	Roberto Caparra Cora Entelman Guillermo Petrocchi Andrea Contegrand Enrique Dieguez Sra Marta Priu	156

architects & designers

Name	Hotel	Page
Ramiro Alatorre	Ikal Del Mar	96
Christina Andrade	Pousada Picinguaba	136
Barry Design Associates	One&Only Ocean Club	68
Architect Luis Bosoms, CEO of Grupo Plan	El Tamarindo	116
Richard Brayton from Brayton + Hughes, San Francisco	Four Seasons Resort Costa Rica	132
Brennan Beer Gorman, Architects, L.L.P.	Mandarin Oriental, New York	60
Avery Brooks & Associates	Four Seasons Resort Great Exuma	64
Roberto Caparra	Palacio Duhau Park Hyatt Buenos Aires	156
Arthur Casas	Emiliano	140
Tony Chi & Associates (restaurant design)	Mandarin Oriental, Miami	56
	Mandarin Oriental, New York	60
Luciano Colombo	The House	92
Andrea Contegrand	Palacio Duhau Park Hyatt Buenos Aires	156
Enrique Dieguez	Palacio Duhau Park Hyatt Buenos Aires	156
Cora Entelman	Palacio Duhau Park Hyatt Buenos Aires	156
Rhoni Epstein	Sagewater Spa	24
Faena Group	Faena Hotel + Universe	152
Oskar Farmer	Cap Juluca	76
Jorge Felly	Kempinski Hotel Colony Park Plaza	146
Janet Gay Freed	Post Ranch Inn	16
Eldin Freeman Team around	Casa Casuarina	44
Jean Michel Gathy	Amanyara	8
Jean Michel Gathy from Denniston International	The Setai	48
Bernardo Gómez-Pimienta	Habita	124
Gordon Campbell Gray	Carlisle Bay	80
Grupo Plan	El Careyes	120
	El Tamarindo	116
Mike Haggerty	Hope Springs	20
Catherine M. Hayes of Hayes	Sanctuary on Camelback Mountain	38
Hill Glazier Architects	One&Only Ocean Club	68
Hirsch Bedner & Associates	Mandarin Oriental, Miami	56
	Mandarin Oriental, New York	60
Hirsch Bedner Associates of Santa Monica, California	St. Regis Resort, Monarch Beach	12
Holmes & Narver of Orange	St. Regis Resort,	
Hiriam Hudson Benedict	Monarch Beach	12
	Sanctuary on Camelback Mountain	38
Jaya Pratomo Ibrahim from Jaya & Associates	The Setai	48
Jensen-Fey Architecture & Planning	W San Diego	34
Jonathan Adler	The Parker Palm Springs	28
Christian Liaigre	Le Sereno	86
Mary Fox Linton	Carlisle Bay	80
David Mann	The Parker Palm Springs	28
Mickey Muennig	Post Ranch Inn	16
Marcello Murzilli	Hotelito Desconocido	112
Enrique Norten	Habita	124
Alfonso Nuñez	Esencia	102
Pascal Arquitectos	Sheraton Centro Histórico	128
Perdian International	One&Only Ocean Club	68
Bob Perkins	Cap Juluca	76
Cristina Pestana	Sagewater Spa	24
Guillermo Petrocchi	Palacio Duhau Park Hyatt Buenos Aires	156
Marta Priu	Palacio Duhau Park Hyatt Buenos Aires	156
Prohotel International	Esencia	102
Kurt Reiner	Pousada Picinguaba	136
Emmanuel Rengade	Pousada Picinguaba	136
RTKL Associates	Mandarin Oriental, Miami	56
Shopworks in collaboration with W Design Group	W San Diego	34
Steve & Misako Samiof	Hope Springs	20
Shawn Hausman and André Balazs Properties	The Standard Miami	52
Smallwood Reynolds Stewart & Stewart	Four Seasons Resort Great Exuma	64
Alison Spear (project architect)	The Standard Miami	52
Philippe Starck	Faena Hotel + Universe	152
TEN Arquitectos	Habita	124
Edward Tuttle	Amangani	8
TX and Art Consultant Joan Warren Grady	Las Ventanas al Paraíso A Rosewood Resort	108
Versace	Casa Casuarina	44
Diego Villasenor	El Careyes	120
Wilson & Associates Dallas	Las Ventanas al Paraíso A Rosewood Resort	108
Xanadu	Cap Juluca	76
Ronald Zürcher of Zürcher Arquitectos	Four Seasons Resort Costa Rica	132

photo credits

Name	Hotel	Page (Photos)
courtesy GHM Hotels	The Setai	Cover
courtesy Amanresorts	Amanyara	Backcover
courtesy Amanresorts	Amangani	8 (all)
	Amanyara	72 (all)
courtesy Cap Juluca	Cap Juluca	76 (all)
courtesy Carlisle Bay	Carlisle Bay	80 (all)
courtesy El Careyes	El Careyes	120 (all)
courtesy El Tamarindo	El Tamarindo	117
courtesy Elegant Hotels	The House	92 (all)
courtesy Faena + Universe	Faena + Universe	153, 154
courtesy GHM Hotels	The Setai	48
courtesy Hotelito Desconocido	Hotelito Desconocido	113, 115
courtesy Hyatt Hotels & Resorts	Palacio Duhau - Park Hyatt Buenos Aires	156 (all)
courtesy Mandarin Oriental Hotel Group	Mandarin Oriental, New York	60, 61, 63
courtesy Sagewater Spa	Sagewater Spa	24 (all)
courtesy Starwood Hotels & Resorts	St. Regis Resort, Monarch Beach	13
	W San Diego	
Katharina Feuer	Faena + Universe	152, 155
Gavin Jackson	Kempinski Hotel Colony Park Plaza	146 (all)
	Emiliano	140 (all)
	Mandarin Oriental, New York	62, 63
	The Parker Palm Springs	28 (all)
	Post Ranch Inn	16 (all)
	Pousada Picinguaba	136 (all)
Nikolas Koenig	Faena + Universe	154 (all)
	The Setai	49, 50, 51
	Sheraton Centro Historico	128-131
	The Standard Miami	52, 54, 55
	St. Regis Resort, Monarch Beach	12, 14, 15
Jean-Philippe Piter	Le Sereno	86 (all)
Undine Pröhl courtesy of HABITA HOTEL	Habita Hotel	124 (all)
Robb Aaron Gordon/ Bernstein & Andriulli	Four Seasons Resort Costa Rica	132 (all

all other photos by
Roland Bauer, Michelle Galindo and Martin Nicholas Kunz

imprint

Bibliographic information published by Die Deutsche Bibliothek. Die Deutsche Bibliothek lists this publication in the Deutsche Nationalbibliografie; detailed bibliographic data are available on the internet at http://ddb.de
ISBN 10: 3-89986-058-6
ISBN 13: 978-3-89986-058-0

Second updated edition
© 2002/2006 Martin Nicholas Kunz
© 2002/2006 fusion publishing gmbh, stuttgart . los angeles
© 2002/2006 avedition GmbH, Ludwigsburg
All rights reserved.

Printed in Austria
by Vorarlberger Verlagsanstalt AG, Dornbirn

Editor | Martin Nicholas Kunz
Editorial coordination | Hanna Engelmeier, Rosina Geiger, Hanna Martin, Patricia Massó, Anne-Kathrin Meier
Copy editing | Gill Kaiser (Ade Team, Stuttgart), Ade Team
Translations | Ade Team, Stuttgart

Layout | Jasmina Bremer
Imaging | Jan Hausberg, Vanessa Kuhn

avedition GmbH
Königsallee 57 | 71638 Ludwigsburg | Germany
p +49-7141-1477391 | f +49-7141-1477399
www.avedition.com | contact@avedition.com

Further information and links at
www.bestdesigned.com
www.fusion-publishing.com

Texts (pages) | Texts by Corina Kayfel (34) and Kerstin Pinger (72, 136, 146, 156). All other texts by fusion publishing. Texts edited by fusion publishing: originals by Patrice Farameh (16, 28, 38, 48, 56, 60, 86, 132), Karin Mahle (52), riva-medien (8, 92) and Ina Sinterhauf (124).

Special thanks to Birgit Abate-Daga, Kempinski Hotels | Sandra Beltran, Prohotel International | Clara Botero, The Setai | Annika Brandenburger, Starwood Hotels & Resorts | Melissa Centeno, St. Regis Resort, Monarch Beach | Leah Corradino, W Hotel San Diego | Rhoni Epstein, Sagewater Spa | Judith Freitag, Rosewood Hotels & Resorts | Martina Frühe ZFL PRCo | Anita Goldmann, Mikulla Goldmann PR | Karin Graf, ZFL PRCo | Simon Heyes, Senderos | Julia Heymann, Trimedia Communications Deutschland GmbH | Annette Hill, Text & Aktion | Sogole Honarvar, bluPRint | Mario J. Leon, MJL Select | Heidi Mayer, Zierer Communications | Rafael Micha, Habita Hotel | Cindy Miller, Elegant Hotels | Feyza Morgül, Uschi Liebl PR | Anjali Nihalchand, Amanresorts | Chloe Peppas, Hope Springs | Victoria Perkins, Sanctuary on Camelback Mountain | Cristina Pestana, Sagewater Spa | María Leonarda Pipkin, Kempinski Hotel Colony Park Plaza | Christian Prieto, Sheraton Centro Histórico | Sue Ricketts, Cap Juluca | Claudia Silva, Hotelito Desconocido | Felipe Silva, Emiliano | Devyani Singh, The Setai | Jonna Sointula, El Careyes | Michael Tavani, Nadine Johnson PR | Liana Vinacur, Palacio Duhau Park Hyatt Buenos Aires | Angie Wade, Casa Casuarina | Lisa Walker, Lisa Walker PR | Vivian Wischt, MJL Select | Patricia Wöhler, Grupo Plan | Bea Wolfe, Passport Resorts | Avon Wong, Amanresorts | Annette Zierer, Zierer Communications for their support.

Martin Nicholas Kunz
1957 born in Hollywood. Founder of fusion publishing creating content for architecture, design, travel, and lifestyle publications.

best designed wellness hotels:
asia pacific
americas
europe
africa & middle east

best designed:
ecological hotels
affordable hotels
modular houses
outdoor living
hotel pools

best designed hotels:
asia pacific
americas
europe I (urban)
europe II (countryside)

All books are released in German and English